WAR OF 1812

GENEALOGY

by

George K. Schweitzer, Ph.D., Sc.D.
407 Ascot Court
Knoxville, TN 37923-5807

Word Processing by

Anne M. Smalley

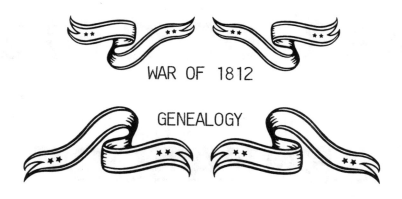

WAR OF 1812

GENEALOGY

ISBN 0-913857-07-6

TABLE OF CONTENTS

Chapter 1

HISTORY OF THE WAR

1. Introduction
Between 18 June 1812 and 16 February 1815, the United States engaged the British in a war which came to be called the War of 1812. At this time the population of the US was approximately 7,700,000 persons and out of them 286,730 men did US military service. These data indicate that about 3.7% of the people were directly involved in the War. Another way of saying this is that about one out of every 27 persons was involved, or about one out of every 14 men. If you had ancestors who were in the US at that time, there is a good chance that one or more of the men was directly involved. These men could be your great-great-great-grandfathers (you had 16) or your great-great-great-great-grandfathers (you had 32), depending on your age. In addition, there would be brothers of these men who might have been involved as well as brothers of the women they married.

At the beginning of the War of 1812 (18 June 1812), the US was made up of the following states and territories: CT, DE, GA, KY, LA, MD, MA (including present day ME), NH, NJ, NY, NC, OH, PA, RI, SC, TN, VA, VT, IN Territory (present day IN), MI Territory (present day MI), IL Territory (present day IL, WI, and eastern MN), MS Territory (present day MS and AL), and LA Territory (present day AR, MO, IA, western MN, ND, SD,NE, KS, OK, MT, eastern WY, and the northeast quarter of CO). The MO Territory was due to be split off from the LA Territory later in the year (01 October 1812). Practically all of present-day FL belonged to Spain which was an ally of Britain during the War.

2. Origins
Even though US independence had been recognized by Great Britain in 1783, the two countries continued to clash. In the areas northwest of the OH River and within the MS Territory, the US was fighting Indians who were being encouraged by the British. In addition, the rise of American commercial shipping was making the US a rival of the British sea trade. In 1793, a long war (until 1815) broke out between France and Britain. Both sides tried to restrict American commercial activity with the other, but since the British ruled the sea lanes, their efforts could be more effective. These efforts constituted the blockading of ports being used for trade with France, demands that American vessels dock at a British port for inspection and payment of fees before proceeding to France, the halting of US ships for examination to determine whether France-bound goods or deserted British seamen were aboard, and the removal of such deserters as well as American seamen from the vessels. By 1810, demands for war

4

for war with Britain were multiplying, especially on the northwestern and southern frontiers where Indian problems were increasing. In addition, the frontier areas were looking at British Canada and Spanish FL (owned by Spain, an ally of Britain) as excellent lands for their expanding populations. In the 1810 Congressional elections, the people (especially those in frontier areas) voted into office many legislators who supported war against Britain. The New England states opposed such a move since their economy was based on sea trade, and they therefore desired peaceful relations with the British.

In the legislative debates of 1811-12, the faction favoring war came to prevail as they made a number of points: (1) the US had been insulted too long by the arrogant British restrictions, (2) US products were rotting because Britain had blocked the markets in Europe, (3) the US economy was suffering because of this lack of sales, (4) Indians were savagely attacking the frontiers, and (5) the means to settle the score could be easily achieved: the invasion and conquest of Canada. In June the Congress declared war and on 18 June 1812 the President signed the declaration. The states of CT, DE, MA, NH, NJ, NY, and RI had voted for peace, but the others had carried the day. On the brink of what one writer calls "this incredible war," the US could list these advantages: (a) Great Britain was heavily involved in the war with France, so could devote little to the conflict, (b) the US was close upon the site of the conflict, while Britain was far away, (c) the US population was much larger than that of Canada, and (d) even though the US Navy was small [16 ships], it was well-trained and well-led. Among the US disadvantages were: (a) a small, ill-trained, poorly-equipped, and poorly-led army, (b) a sizable number of states which opposed the War, (c) the unsolved problem of how strong the central government should be, and (d) the lack of a national bank to finance the conflict so that borrowing through public subscription had to be relied on.

3. The geography of the War

The most important key to understanding the War of 1812 is a knowledge of the geography of the conflict. The aim of the US during most of the combat was to invade and conquer Canada. Therefore, it should not surprise you to know that the US-Canadian border was the scene of much of the action, both on land and on water. In addition, the area surrounding Chesapeake Bay (CB-1) and the region of New Orleans (NO-1) were the sites of other major hostilities, these largely being attempts by the British to capture or raid major US centers. Figure 1 is an outline map of what we now call the eastern portion of the US. The pertinent segment of the Canadian border is that which runs from the Straits of Mackinac (SM-1) southward through Lake Huron (LH-1), then down the centers of the St. Clair River (SR-1), Lake

St. Clair (LS-1), and the Detroit River as it passes just east of Detroit (D-1). The border then moves generally eastward through the middle of Lake Erie (LE-1), then north through the Niagara River (NR-1), passing Buffalo (B-1), then into Lake Ontario (LO-1) eastward down the center of the Lake, then northeasterly down the St. Lawrence River (SL-1) passing Montreal (M-1) to the Atlantic Ocean. The capital letters in parentheses refer to abbreviations on Figure 1, and the number 1 refers you to Figure 1 (page 6).

Figures 2 through 6 provide you with more detailed maps of the major areas: Figure 2 the Detroit area, Figure 3 the Niagara area, Figure 4 the Northern NY area, Figure 5 the Chesapeake Bay area, and Figure 6 the New Orleans area. As battles, military sites, towns, forts, lakes, and rivers are mentioned in this brief history of the War, frequent reference to these simple maps will be of considerable aid to you. As in the previous paragraph, capital letters in parentheses will refer you to abbreviations in the Figure represented by the number in parentheses. For example, (D-2) means to look for the symbol D in Figure 2.

4. The initial year

The basic US strategy for the conduct of the War was for the invasion of Canada by the launching of a threefold attack: (1) in the east, an army was to head for Montreal moving north along the Lake Champlain (LC-4) route in northeastern NY State, (2) in the center, troops were to attack Canada moving west across the Niagara River (NR-3) boundary in northwestern NY State, and (3) in the west, forces were to move east from Detroit (D-2) in the southeastern section of the MI Territory into Upper Canada. President Madison called upon the New England militia to make the advance to Montreal (M-4), but MA and CT denounced the President and refused to send their militia, as did other New England states. Many of these New England states never did wholeheartedly support the invasion and they continued throughout the War to trade with Canada. US General Hull, with about 2200 men, marched to Detroit (D-2), then invaded Canada on 12 July 1812, and entrenched at Sandwich (S-2). While he was there, on 17 July a British landing party surprised the US garrison on Mackinac Island (where Lakes Huron and MI merge) and forced its surrender. Then, on 8 August, Hull pulled back to Detroit (D-2) out of fear that Indians would cut his supply line and out of the failure of OH and MI reinforcements to arrive. British General Brock with 2000 British regulars and Canadian militia convinced Hull that he was outnumbered and in danger of Indian massacre, so he surrendered his entire army on 16 August 1812. On the previous day, 15 August, the US outpost at Fort Dearborn (Chicago) had been massacred. This left the British in uncontested control of Lake Erie (LE-1) and MI.

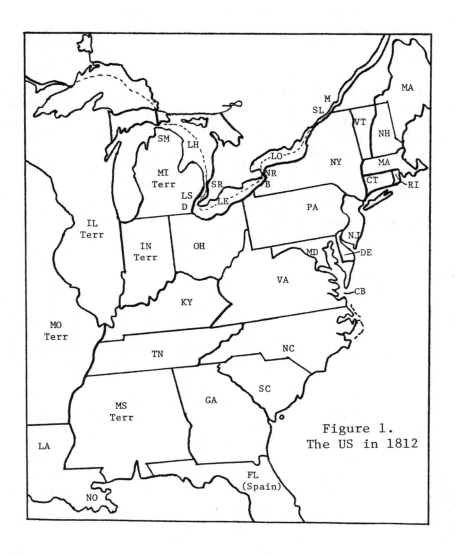

Figure 1.
The US in 1812

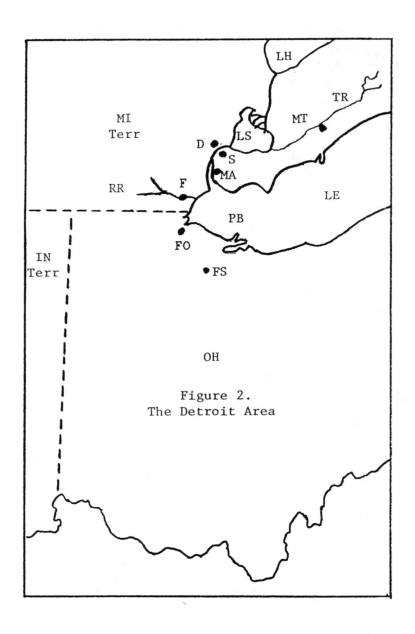

Figure 2.
The Detroit Area

8

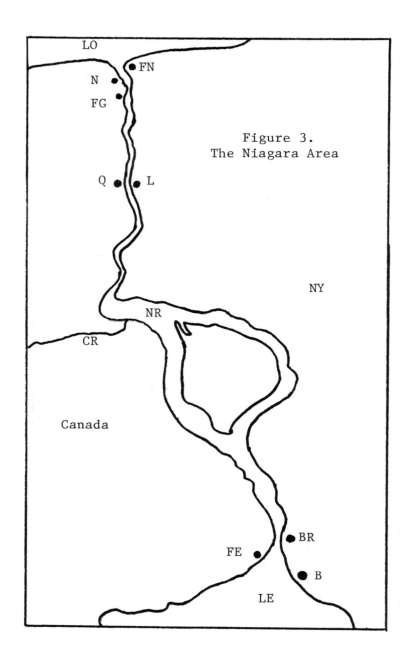

Figure 3.
The Niagara Area

9

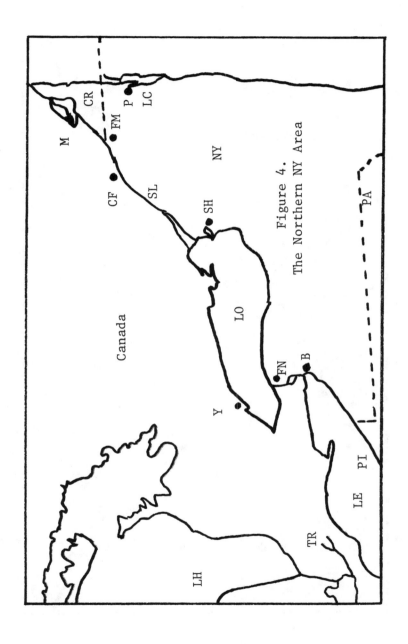

Figure 4.
The Northern NY Area

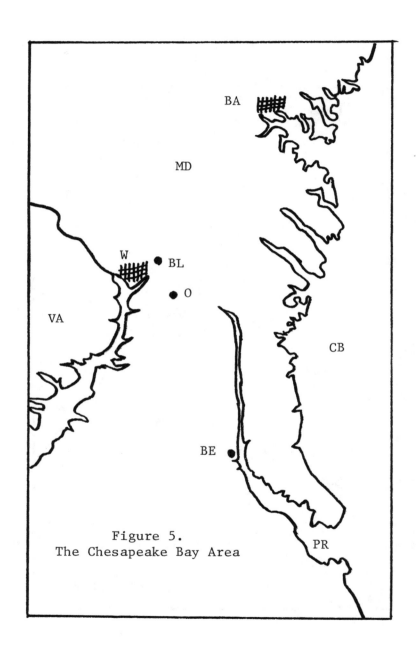

Figure 5.
The Chesapeake Bay Area

11

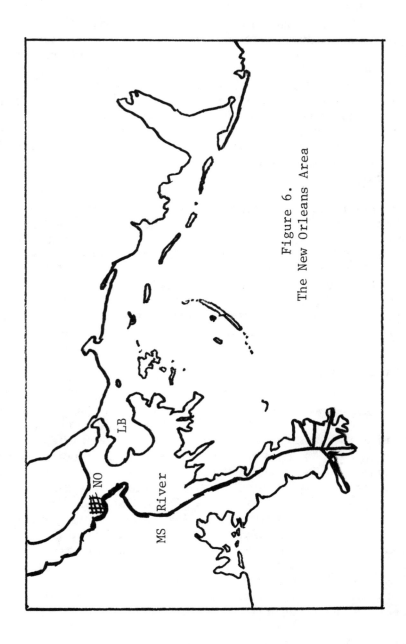

Figure 6.
The New Orleans Area

The British General Brock moved then to Fort George (FG–3), which is on the Canadian side of the Niagara River (NR–3), his arrival occurring on 23 August. Here he faced a US force across the river, these troops being under General Van Rensselaer. The Americans went on the offensive on 13 October when Van Rensselaer sent 600 men to take Queenston Heights ((Q–3). They were overwhelmed by the 1000 British when the NY State Militia refused to leave the state to help them. In November, the largest force of armed Americans yet assembled had gathered at Plattsburg, NY (P–4), under General Dearborn. This force marched north, crossed the border, and engaged a British force. But Dearborn had to withdraw when NY militia again refused to fight outside their state.

In spite of these four dismal performances, the spirits of the country did not become totally despairing, largely because of a number of naval victories. The military impact of these was not great; in fact, they were counterproductive in that they hastened a tight British blockade of the country. However, as morale boosters, they were exceptionally valuable. Among the victories were the US Constitution's defeat of the British Guerriere (19 August), the US Wasp's besting the British Frolic (17 October), the US United States' subdual of the British Macedonian (25 October), and the US Constitution's sinking of the British Java (29 December).

5. The events of 1813

On 26 December 1812 the British announced the blockade of Chesapeake (CB–1) and Delaware Bays (DB–1). These actions marked the beginnings of an evertightening control of the American coastline which kept US ships in port, terminated much trade, and permitted British naval and army forces to make repeated landings to ravage towns and cities along the coast. The initial blockade was extended on 26 May to the mouth of the MS River, New York, Charleston, Port Royal, and Savannah. With the blockade of Long Island Sound on 16 November, only the ports on the New England coast remained open. The British permitted this in the hope that this area of the country might secede and join Canada. However, when this hope grew dim, New England was finally blockaded on 25 April 1814. The blockade was very effective, producing economic distress of sizable proportions. The US sent out cruisers to attack commercial convoys and encouraged privateering, an activity in which private armed vessels captured Britain's merchant ships. Over 1700 had been taken by the end of the War. In fact, the presence of American privateers around British coasts in 1814 made it necessary for practically all shipping to be accompanied by armed vessels. The American efforts did little, however, to loosen the grip of the British stranglehold on the US ports.

When Fort Dearborn (Chicago) and Detroit (D-2) were taken by the British in August of 1812, the US forces fell back into northern OH and IN. The frontier practically everywhere in this area became alive with Indian attacks, the Indians taking advantage of the US defeats. In the fall, numerous counter-raids by US forces resulted in defeats for the Indians. By late September US General Harrison began to move about 6000 men northward with an aim of retaking Detroit (D-2). In the middle of December, one contingent of his held out against British-Indian forces in northern IN, after which they moved back to Detroit (D-2) and Malden (MA-2). On 22 January 1813, General Winchester acting on his own, moved troops to Frenchtown (F-2) on the Raisin River (RR) where British and Indians surprised them. The result was a disastrous defeat, many Americans killed in battle or massacred, and many taken prisoner. The next major action in this Detroit arena was a British-Indian attempt during 1-9 May to dislodge General Harrison from his position at Ft. Meigs (FO-2). The 10-day siege was unsuccessful, as was the 2 August British attack on Ft. Stephenson (FS-2).

On 1 June, the British ship Shannon outgunned, boarded, and captured the US Chesapeake, bringing the frigate into Halifax as a prize. This was a noteworthy incident in that it signaled the final establishment of the tight ME-to-FL British blockade. About three months later, 10 September, to be exact, the most important naval battle on the Great Lakes was to occur. A young naval officer Captain Perry had arrived on 27 March at Presque Isle (PI-4), a peninsula at Erie, PA, on the southeastern shore of Lake Erie (LE-4). Here Perry supervised the building of six warships. While he was hard at work, 1600 US troops under General Dearborn boarded naval vessels under Captain Chauncey at Sackett's Harbor (SH-4) at the eastern end of Lake Ontario (LO-4) and raided York [Toronto] (Y-4) on 27 April. The city surrendered, one ship was captured and one destroyed, and lawless US soldiers burned the public buildings. On 27 May, US General Scott used Chauncey's ships to carry 4000 soldiers to attack the British at Ft. George (FG-4) on the Niagara front, forcing a British evacuation. Their weakened position also caused them to withdraw from Ft. Erie (FE-4), this enabling Captain Perry to take 5 ships from the naval yard at Black Rock (BR-4). In August, Perry moved his fleet of 10 ships to the southwestern end of Lake Erie (LE-2) at Put-In Bay (PB-2). On 9 September a British squadron of 6 ships moved toward Perry's force. The next day in a pitched, bloody battle, Perry defeated the British and gained control of Lake Erie for the US.

When US General Scott took Ft. George (FG-3) and compelled the British to leave Ft. Erie (FE-3) on 27 May, a group of about 2000 troops pursued the fleeing British. The pursuit was halted by a British counter-attack on 6 June at Stoney Creek (SC-3), where the Americans were forced to return to Ft. George (FG-3). The US occupation force shortly left Ft Erie (FE-3), and it was reoccupied by the British. At about this same time, the British attempted to land a sizable force at Sackett's Harbor (SH-4) in order to devastate the US base there. However, the action which took place on 28-29 May was repulsed by the US garrison.

The gaining of control of Lake Erie (LE-1) by Perry on 10 September forced a British evacuation of Detroit (D-2) on 18 September, and permitted US General Harrison to use Perry's ships to land about 4500 infantry near Malden (MA-2) on 27 September. When the British abandoned Malden (MA-2), Harrison pursued them north through Sandwich (S-2), then east to Moravian Town (MT-2) on the Thames River (TR-2). On 5 October, the Battle of the Thames was fought, and Harrison won a stunning victory. In the struggle the Indian leader Tecumseh was killed and as a result, the strong Indian confederacy collapsed and the Indians deserted the British cause. The US thereby regained the Northwest frontier and held it throughout the remainder of the War.

Meanwhile, a second attempt to take Montreal (M-4), which was defended by 15,000 men, was being planned. A combined attack was projected: (1) US General Wilkinson was to move troops by water from Sackett's Harbor (SH-4) down the St. Lawrence River (SL-4) to Montreal (M-4) and (2) US General Hampton was to move north toward Montreal (M-4) from Plattsburg (P-4). On 17 October, Wilkinson left Sackett's Harbor (SH-4) and on 10 November stopped on the Canadian side at Chrysler's Farm (CF-4), 90 miles from Montreal (M-4). On 11 November a British war party came up behind the US forces, and US General Boyd was dispatched with 2000 troops to meet them. The US contingent was routed by the British, and Wilkinson called off the campaign, withdrawing his men across the river to NY, where they went into winter quarters at French Mills (FR-4). The second prong of the Montreal (M-4) attack fared no better under Hampton. He marched his 4000-soldier force to the Canadian line, arriving there on 19 September. Hampton then turned west and camped on the Chateaugay River (CR-4). On 16 October, he moved his troops down river, arriving on 22 October at a point about 14 miles from the river's mouth. His closeness to Montreal (M-4) did not really menace the Canadian city because of Hampton's marked numerical inferiority. After attacking a small British outpost force on 25 October, Hampton abandoned the drive to Montreal (M-4) and returned south to Plattsburg (P-4).

By December, British strength on the Niagara frontier had accumulated to the point where US General McClure prudently evacuated Ft. George (FG-3). Just before his departure, McClure burned the village of Newark (N-3) and a section of Queenston (Q-3). In retaliation, the British captured Ft. Niagara (FN-3) on 18 December and set Indians free to ravage US settlements in the area. For two weeks the Indians gutted a strip of land 36 miles long and 12 miles wide including Lewiston (L–3) (all the way from Lake Erie to Lake Ontario).   Then on 29–30 December British troops burned Buffalo (B–3) and Black Rock (BR–3).

During 1813 there was also combat action in the South which carried over into 1814.   In February, Congress authorized the US takeover of Western FL.   Some of the Indians in the region and north of it (mainly AL) launched a British–encouraged series of attacks on US settlements and outposts.   In October, General Andrew Jackson commanding a force of about 2500 began a series of successful counterattacks.   After loss of many troops by enlistment expirations and desertions, Jackson received reinforcements in January 1814.   On 27 March 1814, Jackson in charge of about 2000 troops dealt an appalling defeat to the Indians as he utterly destroyed them and their stronghold at Horse Shoe Bend, a peninsula made by the Tallapoosa River in west–central AL.   In April, peace came to the areas as the hostile Indians finally surrendered.   In August, a treaty in which the Indians gave up 23 million acres of land was concluded.

6. The events of 1814

As the year 1814 dawned, the complexion of the war was about to change because Napoleon was nearing defeat in Europe.   Upon his capitulation, the British would be free to concentrate upon the hostilities in America, which meant that they could send in reinforcements.   The war, therefore, turned around in that the aim of the US was about to become the defense of its own territory rather than the invasion of Canada.   Fortunately, the American army had been strengthened considerably in the latter half of 1813 and the early months of 1814, both from a standpoint of leadership and competency and training of the soldiers.   The abdication of Napoleon occurred on 6 April 1814.   Shortly thereafter the British began to implement the plans they had been making for attacks upon the US.   These plans called for joint naval–land operations in the areas of Niagara (Figure 3), Lake Champlain (Figure 4), Chesapeake Bay (Figure 5), and New Orleans (Figure 6).

The Niagara campaign had to be abandoned because of the exceptional strength American forces showed in the area.   On 3 July a 3500–man contingent of US soldiers moved across the Niagara River (NR–3) and took Ft. Erie (FE–3).   About 16 miles north of the fort, the retreating British set up their forces on the Chippewa Plain which was backed by a defensive line on the north bank of the river.   US General Scott attacked with a brigade of 1300 men on 5 July.   This force inflicted a stunning defeat on the British.   The British troops were then reinforced and so were the Americans.   On 25 July another major battle unfolded at the village of Lundy's Lane where US General Brown attacked 3000 British troops with 2600 US soldiers. The contest ended in a draw, neither side gaining any advantage, although Brown withdrew after the fighting ceased. As British reinforcements arrived, the Americans moved back to take up a position in Fort Erie. Beginning on 2 August, Ft. Erie came under seige as 3500 British troops entrenched around the fort. On 15 August the defending Americans repulsed an attack producing heavy enemy losses. After another month of seige, US General Porter led 1600 of the troops of the fort in a sortie which destroyed the British seige guns and compelled their withdrawal on 21 September. These military actions in the Niagara arena demonstrated to the British that the Americans could fight toe-to-toe with the best the British could offer. Later in 1814, Ft. Erie was abandoned by the US forces when their hopes of invading Canada had completely died.

British plans for invading the US along the Lake Champlain (LC-4) route lent ominous proportions to the American situation. About 11,000 British veterans along with 4 ships and 12 gunboats hovered just across the border. To meet them, the Americans had only 3300 men plus 4 ships and 10 gunboats under Captain MacDonough. On 31 August the British left Canada and marched along the western edge of Lake Champlain with their supporting fleet not far behind. This large number of British troops drove US General Macomb's much smaller army to a defense position just below Plattsburg (P-4). On 11 September, the enemy fleet engaged the US vessels. The result was a complete American victory involving the seizure or destruction of British ships, the loss of great quantities of British supplies, and the desertion of many British soldiers. The enemy general, deciding he could not risk attack from the rear, and realizing his water supply line had been severed, retreated into Canada. The greatest British threat of the entire war had been turned back.

Unfortunately, British plans for the Chesapeake Bay (CB-5) operations came to be realized to a much greater extent. On 19 August a British expedition which had moved into Chesapeake Bay, then into the Patuxent River (PR-5), was put ashore at Benedict (BE-5). The force of 4000 veterans had three goals in mind: to capture American gunboats in the Patuxent River, to raid Washington, and to attack Baltimore. When the British came up the River, US Admiral Cockburn destroyed the gunboats to prevent their capture. The British troops marched to Marlboro on 22 August, as the Americans gathered militia from neighboring states to defend Washington. About 7000 Americans (a few hundred regulars, 400 sailors, militia) took up a position at Old Fields (O-5) about 8 miles south of Bladensburg (BL-5). The US defenders were routed on 24 August by the enemy, who marched on to the outskirts of Washington (W-5) where they set up camp. On that day and the morning of 25 August, the British set fire to the Capitol, the White House, most of the departmental buildings, the office of the newspaper The National Intelligencer, and several houses, and the Americans destroyed the Navy Yard. On the night of 25 August, the British forces took to their ships.

On 12 September, another British expedition landed at North Point (NP-5) and began to move toward Baltimore (BA-5). The city itself was defended by about 13,000 soldiers and the harbor was defended by about 100 men who occupied Ft. McHenry. The British land advance was temporarily checked outside Baltimore by 3200 militia and severe casualties were inflicted on the British, including the mortal wounding of their general. The enemy then continued to march until they arrived near the heavily defended heights of Baltimore on 13 September. When the British fleet's two-day bombardment failed to subdue Fort McHenry (the Star-spangled Banner yet waved as Frances Scott Key watched o'er the ramparts), the invaders withdrew and boarded their ships. After hovering in Chesapeake Bay (CB-5) for about a month, the expedition sailed for Jamaica.

7. The end of the War

In May of 1814, US General Jackson had been made commander of the military district of the Mobile-New Orleans area. After going to Pensacola to seize that Spanish FL town which was a British base, Jackson left Mobile and arrived at New Orleans (NO-6) on 1 December. When he realized the British were moving to assault New Orleans and take control of the MS River, he headquartered his troops at Baton Rouge. When over 50 British ships approached Lake Borque (LB-6) on 13 December, the Americans speedily moved to that town. On 16 December, the British began disembarking their 14,000 troops on the shores of the Lake, finishing on 23 December. As they initiated their advance on New Orleans, Jackson led a night attack on them (23-24 December) which delayed their movement. About five miles from New Orleans, he then built a line of fortifications across the enemy's path. On 8 January 1815 the main British force of 5300 attacked the 4500 entrenched US troops. In the slaughter that ensued three British generals were killed and over 2000 soldiers were killed or wounded. On 27 January the British took ship and departed. All of this action occurred after a peace treaty had been signed by the US and Britain in Ghent, Belgium on 24 December. The battle proceeded because the news had reached neither of the forces at New Orleans. Peace negotiations had been going on for quite sometime; in fact they had begun in August of 1814. The British were pressing to retain all the territories they occupied at the time, whereas the US envoys were holding out for a return to the situation as it was at the beginning of the war. American victories during the fall, the growing opposition of the British public to continuing the conflict, and the advice of several leading British officials led the government of Britain to accede to the American proposal. The treaty was signed on 24 December 1814, news of it reached New York City on 11 February 1815, and on 17

February it was ratified by the Senate. The treaty provided for essentially nothing but a cessation of warfare. However, several notable changes occurred including: (l) never again did a British warship stop a US vessel and take an American seaman, (2) the war broke the power of Indians in the northwest and the south, and thus permitted rapid expansion into these areas, (3) the way was paved for the purchase of FL from Spain in 1819, (4) the war gave the US a renewed national spirit of independence, and (5) the blockade of the US had begun a commercial and industrial independence which was to expand rapidly.

8. US Regiments The US regiments which served in the War of 1812 will be listed in this section. It is very important that you recognize that not all the men who fought in the War of 1812 were enlisted in federal (US) regiments. Many fought as members of state militia units which were never incorporated into the federal military system. Their records did not usually make it into the federal record-keeping organizations, which means that their records remained with the individual states. In many instances, these militia records are not very extensive.

The US regiments which were active during the War years are listed here. First, their names will be given, then where the men in them were raised, and finally the battles in which they were engaged.
_1st RIFLE REGIMENT (men from LA, MS Territory, KY, OH, IN Territory, NY, VT). Fought at Gannonoque (21 Sep 1812), Elizabeth-town (07 Feb 1813), Ogdensburg (22 Feb 1813), York (27 Apr 1813), Fort George (27 May 1813), Stoney Creek (06 Jun 1813), Hoople's Creek, Massequoi Village (12 Oct 1813), LaColle Mill (30 Mar 1814), Sandy Creek (30 May 1814), Conjockta Creek (03 Aug 1814), Fort Erie (03 Jul 1814), Plattsburg (11 Sep 1814), and some of them at Point Petre (13 Jan 1815).
_2nd RIFLE REGIMENT (men from OH and TN). Involved in no battles.
_3rd RIFLE REGIMENT (men from VA, NC, SC). Involved in no battles.
_4th RIFLE REGIMENT (men from PA). Fought at Fort Erie (03 Jul 1814), Cook's Mills (19 Oct 1814).
_1st INFANTRY (men from NJ). Fought at Brownstown (05 Aug 1812), Fort Dearborn (15 Aug 1812), Fort Wayne (04 Sep 1812), Detroit (16 Aug 1812), Campbell's Island (19 Jul 1814), Lundy's Lane (25 Jul 1814), Fort Erie (03 Jul 1814).
_2nd INFANTRY (men from LA). Fought at Fort Bowyer (11 Feb 1815).
_3rd INFANTRY (men from MS Territory). Fought at Eccanachaca (23 Dec 1813), Pensacola (07 Nov 1814).

__4th INFANTRY (men from NH). Fought at Brownstown (05 Aug 1812), Detroit (16 Aug 1812), Chateaugay (25-26 Oct 1813), French-man's Creek (01 Nov 1813), LaColle Mill (30 Mar 1814), Plattsburg (11 Sep 1814).

__5th INFANTRY (men from PA). Fought at Stoney Creek (06 Jun 1813), Frenchman's Creek (01 Nov 1813), Chateaugay (25-26 Oct 1813), LaColle Mill (30 Mar 1814), Chippewa (05 Jul 1814), Cook's Mills (19 Oct 1814).

__6th INFANTRY (men from NY). Fought at Queenston Heights (13 Oct 1812), York (27 Apr 1813), Fort George (27 May 1813), Beaver Dams (24 Jun 1813), Frenchman's Creek (01 Nov 1813), LaColle Mill (30 Mar 1814), Plattsburg (11 Sep 1814).

__7th INFANTRY (men from KY). Fought at Fort Harrison (05 Sep 1812), Prairie du Chien (19 Jul 1814), Rock River (05 Sep 1814), New Orleans (08 Jan 1815), Fort St. Philip (09 Jan 1815).

__8th INFANTRY (men from GA). Involved in no battles.

__9th INFANTRY (men from MA). Fought at Sackett's Harbor (29 May 1813), Chrysler's Farm (11 Nov 1813), Chippewa (05 Jul 1814), Lundy's Lane (25 Jul 1814), Fort Erie (03 Jul 1814).

__10th INFANTRY (men from NC). Fought at Chateaugay (25-26 Oct 1813), LaColle Mill (30 Mar 1814).

__11th INFANTRY (men from VT). Fought at Chrysler's Farm (11 Nov 1813), LaColle Mill (30 Mar 1814), Chippewa (05 Jul 1814), Lundy's Lane (25 Jul 1814), Fort Erie (03 Jul 1814).

__12th INFANTRY (men from VA). Fought at Black Rock (11 Jul 1813), Chrysler's Farm (11 Nov 1813), LaColle Mill (30 Mar 1814), Odletown (28 Jun 1814), Bladensburg (24 Aug 1814).

__13th INFANTRY (men from NY). Fought at Queenston Heights (13 Oct 1812), Black Rock (11 Jul 1813), Fort George (27 May 1813), Chrysler's Farm (11 Nov 1813), LaColle Mill (30 Mar 1814), Plattsburg (11 Sep 1814).

__14th INFANTRY (men from MD). Fought at Fort Niagara (21 Nov 1813), Black Rock (28 Nov 1812), Fort George (27 May 1813), Beaver Dams (24 Jun 1813), Chrysler's Farm (11 Nov 1813), LaColle Mill (30 Mar 1814), Cook's Mills (19 Oct 1814).

__15th INFANTRY (men from NJ). Fought at York (27 Apr 1813), Fort George (27 May 1813), Frenchman's Creek (01 Nov 1813), Chrysler's Farm (11 Nov 1813), LaColle Mill (30 Mar 1814), Cook's Mills (19 Oct 1814).

__16th INFANTRY (men from PA). Fought at York (27 Apr 1813), Fort George (27 May 1813), Stoney Creek (06 Jun 1813), Chrysler's Farm (11 Nov 1813), Cook's Mills (19 Oct 1814).

__17th INFANTRY (men from KY). Fought at River Raisin (22 Jan 1813), Fort Meigs (28 Apr-08 May 1813), Fort Stephenson (02 Aug 1813), Mackinac (04 Aug 1814).

__18th INFANTRY (men from SC). Involved in no battles.

__19th INFANTRY (men from OH). Fought at Detroit (16 Aug 1812), Mississinewa (17 Dec 1812), River Raisin (22 Jan 1813), Fort Meigs (28 Apr–04 May 1813), Fort Niagara (18 Dec 1813), Mackinac (04 Aug 1814), Chippewa (05 Jul 1814), Lundy's Lane (25 Jul 1814), Fort Erie (03 Jul 1814).

__20th INFANTRY (men from VA). Fought at Black Rock (28 Nov 1812), Fort George (27 May 1813), LaColle Mill (30 Mar 1814).

__21st INFANTRY (men from MA). Fought at York (27 Apr 1813), Fort George (27 May 1813), Sackett's Harbor (29 May 1813), Chrysler's Farm (11 Nov 1813), Chippewa (05 Jul 1814), Lundy's Lane (25 Jul 1814), Fort Erie (03 Jul 1814).

__22nd INFANTRY (men from PA). Fought at Fort Niagara (21 Nov 1812), Fort George (27 May 1813), Frenchman's Creek (01 Nov 1813), Chrysler's Farm (11 Nov 1813), Chippewa (05 Jul 1814), Lundy's Lane (25 Jul 1814), Fort Erie (03 Jul 1814).

__23rd INFANTRY (men from NY). Fought at Queenston Heights (13 Oct 1812), Black Rock (28 Nov 1812), Fort George (27 May 1813), Sackett's Harbor (29 May 1813), Stoney Creek (06 Jun 1813), Beaver Dams (24 Jun 1813), LaColle Mill (30 Mar 1814), Chippewa (05 Jul 1814), Lundy's Lane (25 Jul 1814), Fort Erie (03 Jul 1814).

__24th INFANTRY (men from TN). Fought at Fort Stephenson (02 Aug 1813), Longwoods (04 Mar 1814), Mackinac (04 Aug 1814).

__25th INFANTRY (men from CT). Fought at Stoney Creek (06 Jun 1813), Chateaugay (25–26 Oct 1813), Chrysler's Farm (11 Nov 1813), Chippewa (05 Jul 1814), Lundy's Lane (25 Jul 1814), Fort Erie (03 Jul 1814).

__26th INFANTRY (men from VT). Fought at Longwoods (04 Mar 1814), Fort Erie (03 Jul 1814).

__27th INFANTRY (men from NY). Fought at Chatham (04 Oct 1813), Thames (05 Oct 1813), Longwoods (04 Mar 1814).

__28th INFANTRY (men from KY). Fought at Longwoods (04 Mar 1814), Sturgeon Creek (05 Jul 1814).

__29th INFANTRY (men from NY). Fought at Chateaugay (25–26 Oct 1813), Plattsburg (11 Sep 1814).

__30th INFANTRY (men from VT). Fought at LaColle Mill (30 Mar 1814), Plattsburg (11 Sep 1814).

__31st INFANTRY (men from VT). Fought at Chateaugay (25–26 Oct 1813), LaColle Mill (30 Mar 1814), Plattsburg (11 Sep 1814).

__32nd INFANTRY (men from DE and PA). Involved in no battles.

__33rd INFANTRY (men from MA). Fought at Chateaugay (25–26 Oct 1813), LaColle Mill (30 Mar 1814), Plattsburg (11 Sep 1814).

__34th INFANTRY (men from MA). Fought at Chateaugay (25–26 Oct 1813), Plattsburg (11 Sep 1814).

__35th INFANTRY (men from VA). Involved in no battles.

__36th INFANTRY (men from MD and VA). Fought at Bladensburg (24 Aug 1814), Fort McHenry (13–14 Sep 1814).

__37th INFANTRY (men from CT). Involved in no battles.

__38th INFANTRY (men from MD). Fought at Bladensburg (24 Aug 1814), Fort McHenry (13-14 Sep 1814).

__39th INFANTRY (men from TN). Fought at Horseshoe Bend (27 Mar 1814).

__40th INFANTRY (men from MA). Fought at Fort Sullivan (in Maine), Pensacola (07 Nov 1814).

__41st INFANTRY (men from NY). Involved in no battles.

__42nd INFANTRY (men from PA and NY). Involved in no battles.

__43rd INFANTRY (men from NC). Fought at Point Petre (13 Jan 1815).

__44th INFANTRY (men from LA). Fought at Pensacola (07 Nov 1814), New Orleans (08 Jan 1815).

__45th INFANTRY (men from MA). Involved in no battles.

__46th INFANTRY (men from NY). Involved in no battles.

9. Recommended reading

The above account of the War of 1812 is only a brief outline, meant simply to acquaint you with the general progress of the conflict. It mentions only the major battles, many others being fought in between these chief encounters. Should you want to do more detailed reading which will strongly enhance your understanding of your ancestor and your search for his records, it is recommended that you begin with two or three treatments longer than the above, but not book length. Among the more suitable materials for this are the following:

_S. E. Morrison, H. S. Commager, and W. E. Leuchtenburg, THE GROWTH OF THE AMERICAN REPUBLIC, Oxford, New York, NY, 1969, volume 1, pages 357-86.

_C. M. Dollar, J. R. Gunderson, R. N. Satz, H. V. Nelson, Jr., and G. Reichard, AMERICA: CHANGING TIMES, Wiley, New York, NY, 1979, volume 1, pages 217-232.

_G. Gurney, A PICTORIAL HISTORY OF THE US ARMY, Crown, New York, NY, 1979, pages 97-122.

_T. H. Williams, THE HISTORY OF AMERICAN WARS, Knopf, New York, NY, 1981, pages 93-134.

_R. Leckie, THE WARS OF AMERICA, Harper and Row, New York, NY, 1981, pages 219-313.

_M. Matloff, editor, AMERICAN MILITARY HISTORY, US Army, Washington, DC, 1969, pages 122-147.

Following your acquaintance with several of the above sources, you may go further by delving into one or more of the better one-volumed treatments of the War of 1812. Recommended are:

_J. K. Mahon, THE WAR OF 1812, University of FL Press, Gainesville, FL, 1972.

22

_H. L. Coles, THE WAR OF 1812, University of Chicago Press, Chicago, IL, 1965.
_F. F. Bierne, THE WAR OF 1812, Dutton and Co., New York, NY, 1949.
_J. R. Jacobs and G. Tucker, THE WAR OF 1812, COMPACT HISTORY, Hawthorne Books, New York, NY, 1969.
_R. Horsman, THE WAR OF 1812, Knopf, New York, NY, 1969.
_J. M. Hitsman, THE INCREDIBLE WAR OF 1812, University of Toronto Press, Toronto, Canada, 1965. [From the Canadian standpoint]
_K. Caffrey, THE TWILIGHT'S LAST GLEAMING, Stein and Day, New York, NY, 1977.
_D. R. Hickey, THE WAR OF 1812, A FORGOTTEN CONFLICT, University of IL Press, Urbana, IL, 1989.

For those who care to go much deeper in the history of the War of 1812 or portions of it, several multivolumed sets are available. Among them you will find:

_G. Tucker, POLTROONS AND PATRIOTS, A POPULAR ACCOUNT OF THE WAR OF 1812, Bobbs–Merrill, Indianapolis, IN, 1954, 2 volumes.
_A. T. Mahan, SEA POWER AND ITS RELATIONS TO THE WAR OF 1812, Little, Brown, and Co., Boston, MA, 1905, 2 volumes.
_J. T. Headley, THE SECOND WAR WITH ENGLAND, New York, NY, 1853, 2 volumes.

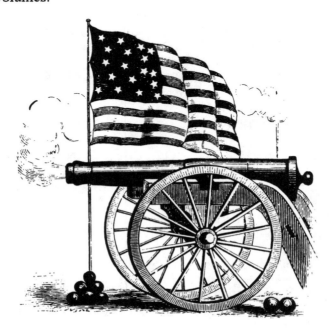

23

Chapter 2

SERICE RECORDS

1. The original records

The War of 1812 generated a large volume of records. Fortunately a sizable portion of them contain genealogical information on more than 280,000 military participants who fought on the US side. In addition, the original records and records derived from them refer to hundreds of thousands of wives, descendants, and associates of these veterans.

During the two-and-one-half-year war, records included enlistment papers, muster rolls, pay rolls, attendance lists, regimental rosters, descriptive lists, account books (on clothing, weapons, and rations issued), and discharge papers. The records contain such items as name, rank, date, organization, enlistment date, term of service, promotions, reasons for absence (illness, wounds, death, missing, desertion, furlough, discharge), birth place and date, place of civilian residence, civilian occupation, height, age, color of eyes and hair, and sometimes a signature. Rarely will all of these be available for a given soldier, sailor, or marine, but many will usually be.

In addition to the above, there were regimental orderly books (records of orders given regiments by superior officers), communications between commanding officers (campaign plans, orders to lower officers, battle reports, lists of wounded and killed, lists of deserters, lists of prisoners), and pertinent records of towns, cities, counties, states, and of the US Congress. Quite a number of the participants kept diaries or journals and wrote letters which have survived.

After the war, even more records were generated. Many of the participants in the conflict had been promised land (called bounty land) for their services, others were awarded bounty land later, and many were owed back pay. A number of civilians were also owed money for services or supplies they provided to the military forces. The civilians and the veterans or their heirs filed claims for these debts with the states or the US Government, the claims were acted upon, and payment records were kept. Further, following the end of the war by quite some years, pensions were awarded to veterans, their wives, and/or their heirs. These actions generated pension applications, decisions on the applications, pension payments, pension alterations as the laws changed, and pension terminations. Pension applications can be of exceptional value genealogically because they contain detailed information in an attempt by the applicant to establish his or her eligibility. Items such as the following are often found: name, rank, state, military unit, dates of enlistment and discharge, birth place and date, amount of pension, places of residence to which the pension was sent, soldier's proof of military service, names of his officers and comrades, battle descriptions, date of death, widow's birth date and place, marriage date and place, names of their children and their birth dates, death date and place of widow, and affidavits of acquaintances, officials, and fellow soldiers. Applicants sometimes went into considerable detail regarding their war experiences. Again, sizable volumes of records were involved. Such was also the case with bounty land applications and the documents that recorded the disposition of them. As you can imagine, some veterans made speeches, wrote articles, or even composed books describing their wartime adventures. A fair number of these are available and often contain useful information on many persons who were in the same organization as the writer.

Most of the original records mentioned above are to be found in the National Archives in Washington, DC. Some will be located in the State Archives in the states that were in existence in 1812-5, in private archives in those states, in city and county records, and in Canadian and British collections. The service records will be discussed in this chapter and you will be told precisely how to find those relating to your War of 1812 ancestor. Other records, including bounty land and pension, will be treated in chapters to follow.

2. Basic types of service

In the War of 1812 there were several categories of personnel who engaged in military activity. It is important to know about these categories because the location of the records on each of them is different. The six basic categories of servicemen participating in the conflict were: (1) members of the volunteer US Army, (2) members of the regular US Army, (3) members of the US Navy, (4) members of the US Marines, (5) members of state or territorial militia organizations who were never made members of the volunteer US Army, and (6) unofficial or semi-official (city, county, region) groups of private citizens who acted against the British or their Indian or Spanish allies.

As you will recall from Chapter 1, about 287,000 participated in the War of 1812 as Federal (US) forces (categories 1-4). Some remarks about each category and the sources of records for them are in order. (1) The volunteer US Army was made up of soldiers who joined the US forces in the war crisis of 1812-5. They were often members of previously-existing state and territorial militia units which were transferred to Federal service. At other times they were raised in the states and territories when the Federal call came for them. They were then constituted as state militia and subsequently transferred to US service. By far the large majority of servicemen in the War of 1812 fell into this category, which means it is the most likely place to look for an ancestor. The service records of these men are in the National Archives. (2) The regular US Army was composed of professional soldiers who made the military their career and served continuously in the permanently organized US Army, both in peace and in war. The National Archives has their records, too. (3) The US Navy and (4) The US Marines were made up of servicemen who enlisted directly in those branches of the military. The service records of men in these organizations (US Navy and US Marines) are also in the National Archives.

(5) At the time of the War of 1812, each state and territory maintained a militia. This was an organization of properly-qualified male citizens which was trained for emergencies such as insurrection, invasion, and outbreaks of lawlessness. In some states, such as MA and CT, these organizations were strong, welltrained, and well-equipped, but in most, they were not. As we have noted above, some state and territorial militia units became parts of the volunteer US Army. Others guarded cities, harbors, towns, and other areas of their own states against invasion. Most remained on call by the state's governor in case they should be needed. A few of these units which did not enter the US service engaged in a bit of active battle service, but most engaged in none. The records of these militia units will be found in state archives, private archives (mostly in the states involved in the War), and in county and city records. These records, as one might expect, are not as thorough as those of the US forces. (6) Finally, there were the unofficial, quasi-official, and semi-official groups which saw combat action in the War. Chief among these were privateers, armed ships owned by private persons which might or might not have government sanction to attack and capture enemy ships. There were also a few civilian groups which gave military service especially when British marauders would invade coastal cities, towns, and areas. In addition, civilians often pitched in and aided militia in times of impending attack, and lent them support during attack, seige, or counteraction. Records of these activities are widely scattered and quite incomplete, but some will be found in practically everyplace mentioned previously: The National Archives, state archives, private archives, and county and city records. In addition, contemporary newspaper accounts often are of considerable value.

Since about one out of every fourteen men in the US at the time of the War of 1812 was involved, you should strongly entertain the possibility that any ancestor of yours who was 13 or greater in 1812 (any man born before 1800) could very well have fought. Records should be sought for every possibility. The major types of records which should be looked for are service records, bounty land records, and pension records, but there are a number of others which must not be overlooked if you want to get the full picture on your veteran ancestor. The remainder of this book will tell you how to go about searching for all these records.

---

3. The volunteer US Army

The large majority of the participants in the War of 1812 were those state militia citizen-soldiers who were taken into the volunteer US Army. The key to their service records is a large microfilm index:

_US Department of War, INDEX TO COMPILED SERVICE RECORDS OF VOLUNTEER SOLDIERS WHO SERVED DURING THE WAR OF 1812, National Archives, Washington, DC, Microfilm Publication M602, 234 rolls.

You should look into this index for every possible ancestor who might have been involved in the War. This means your direct male ancestors, their brothers, and the brothers of your direct female ancestors. This index lists for each participating soldier his state and his military organization, or in the case of a small percent of the soldiers, his non-state organization. This index is not only in the National Archives [PA Avenue between 7th and 9th Streets, NW, Washington, DC 20408], but copies are also available in some state libraries, some state archives, some large genealogical libraries, and some of the regional branches of the National Archives. State libraries, state archives, and genealogical libraries are listed in the most widely-circulated genealogical journal and in two convenient compendia:

_V. N. Chambers, editor, THE GENEALOGICAL HELPER, Everton Publishers, Logan, UT, latest May-June issue.
_E. P. Bentley, THE GENEALOGIST'S ADDRESS BOOK, Genealogical Publishing Co., Baltimore, MD, latest edition.
_A. Eichholz, ANCESTRY'S RED BOOK, Ancestry, Salt Lake City, UT, latest edition.

The regional branches of the National Archives are located in or near Boston [Waltham], New York, Philadelphia, Chicago, Atlanta [East Point], Kansas City, Fort Worth, Denver, San Francisco [San Bruno], Los Angeles [Laguna Niguel], and Seattle. They may be located by looking in the telephone directories under US GOVERNMENT-FEDERAL ARCHIVES AND RECORDS CENTER.

Once you have located an ancestor in the microfilm indexes, your next step will be to obtain his service record. These records are filed in the National Archives (Record Group 94, Entry 510). They consist of cards placed in a file envelope. Most envelopes are arranged by name of the state, then by the name of the military unit, then alphabetically by the name of the soldier. For those soldiers who served in non-state units [Indian regiments, prisoners, Quartermaster Department, spies, etc.], the envelopes are arranged by unit, then alphabetically by the name of the soldier. Generally, the records will give the soldier's state, his rank, his military organization, when he was mustered in, and when he was discharged. Sometimes the soldier's age, place of birth, and place of enlistment will also be shown. Information on the soldier will have been obtained from records such as muster rolls, inspection reports, hospital lists, deserter lists, and other such documents.

In addition to these service records, there are in the National Archives two other less important groups of records. Neither of these groups of records carries much genealogical data, but if you want to do a thorough job of completing a service record, they may be consulted. The first group is Muster Rolls of Volunteer Organizations (Record Group 94, Entry 55). These muster rolls are arranged by state, and then under each state by numerical order of regiment and/or by name of commanding officer. You will have learned your veteran's state and regiment (either number or commander) from the microfilm index (M602), therefore you can locate muster rolls in this group of records. The second group is usually referred to as Miscellaneous Records of 1812-5 (Record Group 94, Entry 125). The miscellaneous records are composed chiefly of information regarding payment of volunteer servicemen and are made up of payment lists, papers, receipts, and correspondence. The records, which carry the soldier's name, rank, military organization, and payment dates are filed in numbered envelopes. There is an index to these envelopes which is arranged alphabetically by the soldier's name (Record Group 94, Entry 126).

The best procedure for obtaining these records is to visit a place that has the microfilm service record index (M602) and look for all your ancestors in it or to hire a researcher to do the work for you. Researchers are listed in:
_V. N. Chambers, editor, THE GENEALOGICAL HELPER, Everton
   Publishers, Logan, UT, latest September-October issue.
Then, if you find one or more ancestors, go to the National Archives or hire a researcher to go and do three things: (1) copy the service records, (2) check the Muster Rolls and the Miscellaneous Record index, and if materials are found, (3) copy out the records. An alternative procedure is to request records from the National Archives using their Form NATF-80, but response is often slow and their fees are only slightly less than a researcher can be hired for. Even so, if you care to proceed by this route, request Form NATF-80 from them [PA Avenue between 7th and 9th Streets, NW, Washington, DC 20408].

4. The regular US Army

It is estimated that somewhat over 50,000 soldiers served in the regular US Army during the hostilities of 1812-5. Thus if an ancestor of yours did not appear in the volunteer listings, he may turn up here. The military service records for enlisted men and for officers of the regular US Army are to be found in separate places.

Thus, the first move you should make is to find out if your ancestor was an officer or not. This can be done readily by consulting a reference volume which lists all regular Army officers during the period 1789-1903. The book, of course, includes officers in the War of 1812:

_F. B. Heitman, HISTORICAL REGISTER AND DICTIONARY OF THE US ARMY, Government Printing Office, Washington, DC, 1903, volume 1, pages 147-1069.

Under the name of each officer the organization(s) to which he belonged is (are) listed. This reference work is present in many state libraries and large genealogical libraries. Should you find an ancestor in it, then you can obtain his records from the National Archives by going there in person, hiring a researcher to go there, or by a mail request. The service records for regular Army officers during 1812-5 must be sought in several places. The search is simplified by the information discovered in Heitman's book. Three sets of microfilms should be examined:

_US Adjutant General's Office, REGISTERS OF ENLISTMENTS IN THE US ARMY, 1798-1914, National Archives Microfilm Publication M233, Washington, DC, 47 rolls. Check volumes 1-35 which are in alphabetical order.

_US Adjutant General's Office, LETTERS RECEIVED BY THE OFFICE OF THE ADJUTANT GENERAL, 1805-21, National Archives Microfilm Publication M566, Washington, DC, 144 rolls. Arranged by year then alphabetical by name.

_US Adjutant General's Office, LETTERS SENT BY THE OFFICE OF THE ADJUTANT GENERAL, 1800-90, National Archives Microfilm Publication M565, Washington, DC, 63 rolls. Index in each of the volumes.

Then, there are four registers and a roster relating to commissioned officers which should be examined. These are in Record Group 94, entries 309, 312, 320, 321, and 323.

If your ancestor was neither a member of the volunteer US Army or an officer in the regular US Army, he could have served as an enlisted man in the regular US Army. The key to the service records of these men is a microfilm set published by the National Archives:

_REGISTER OF ENLISTMENTS IN THE US ARMY, 1798-1914, National Archives, Washington, DC, Microfilm Publication M233, 69 rolls (61-8 restricted).

The first 13 reels cover the years 1793-1815 which includes the War of 1812 period. The records in these first 13 reels are arranged alphabetically or alphabetically to the first letter of the given name. Care must be used in looking for persons in them since the listings may not be strictly alphabetical. In other words, you should look carefully through the entire section pertaining to the first letter of your ancestor's surname. The records are summaries of data in enlistment documents, inspection records, muster rolls, and other similar papers. They are often incomplete, but usually show name, date and place and term of enlistment, birth place, regiment and company, and date of discharge. Since these records are often incomplete, one other collection may be investigated to fill in missing details: Enlistment Papers (Record Group 94, Entry 91) [look under initial letter of surname for folder]. Items which may be found in these documents are age, occupation, enlistment data, reenlistment information, personal descriptions, death report, burial place, and disabilities. Again the general procedures for obtaining these records (personal visit, or hiring a researcher, or mail request) are the same as described in the last paragraph of section 3 of this chapter.

5. The US Navy

Quite a number of men served in the US Navy in the War of 1812, the two major naval arenas being the Atlantic Ocean and the Great Lakes, although the Gulf of Mexico also saw action. As you will remember from the historical chapter, there was also naval action in upper NY state, principally on Lake Champlain. As was the case for the regular Army, records for commissioned officers and enlisted men must be sought separately since they are in slightly different areas in the National Archives.

Your first approach will be to see if your ancestor is listed in the following alphabetical compilation of naval officers who served during the period 1775–1900. Included are those who participated in the War of 1812.

_E. W. Callahan, LIST OF OFFICERS OF THE NAVY OF THE US AND OF THE MARINE CORPS FROM 1775 TO 1900, Haskell House, New York, NY, 1901, pages 15–609.

If you find your ancestor or a person who you believe is your ancestor in the Callahan compilation, you then should look him up in the microfilmed records of naval officers:

_Department of the Navy, ABSTRACTS OF SERVICE RECORDS OF NAVAL OFFICERS, National Archives Microfilm M330, Washington, DC, 19 rolls.

This microfilm set is a copy of 15 volumes labelled A through O. Two of the volumes list abstracts of service records of officers in the War of 1812, volumes D and E. The entries are either alphabetical or are indexed. An entry will usually give data obtained from appointment, assignment, transfer, promotion, and resignation documents such as dates of these actions, changes in ranks, and ships on which he served. If you really want to push your investigation to its limits you may look into several series of Letters from Officers (Record Group 45, Entries 65, 66, and 67).

If you did not find your ancestor in Callahan (indicating he was not a commissioned officer), then you should look into the service records of <u>enlisted men</u>. <u>First,</u> take a look at the microfilms referred to in the previous paragraph, because there are also some noncommissioned officers listed in them. <u>Then,</u> you will need to make an arduous search through the Muster and Pay Rolls of Ships and of Shore Establishments (Record Group 45, Entries 90 and 92). Unfortunately, these are not indexed. They are arranged in bound volumes under the name of the ship or the shore establishment, and then chronologically. Of course, you will need only to go through those for 1812-5, but there are lots of entries. Information usually included consists of name, date of arrival, date of service, ship or shore establishment from which he came and to which he went. If one could find out the ship or shore establishment for an ancestor by some other means, this search could be simplified greatly. The two major ways to do this are through bounty land and pension records. These will be discussed in the next chapter, and it is recommended that you take that approach before you try going through ship and shore establishment rolls entry-by-entry. Once you know the ship or shore establishment, then you can personally look into these records, or hire a researcher to do so, or correspond with the National Archives (for general procedure, see last paragraph, section 3, this chapter).

6. The US Marine Corps

A number of men did service in the US Marine Corps during the War of 1812. Their records may be considered to fall into two groups: those relating to officers, and those relating to enlisted men.

If you suspect that your ancestor was a Marine <u>officer</u>, look him up in the following volume:

_E. W. Callahan, LIST OF OFFICERS OF THE NAVY OF THE US AND OF THE MARINE CORPS FROM 1775 TO 1900, Haskell House, New York, NY, 1901, pages 679-701.

Should you find your forebear in this listing, you will need to dig into two files in the National Archives. The first is the Card Record of Officers. This card file is arranged alphabetically by the first several letters of the last name, then by the given name. On the card of a given officer will be found his rank and year of appointment. The second file you should examine is the Letters of Acceptance (Record Group 80, Entry 45) which are arranged in several volumes. The volume for 1808-16 is arranged alphabetically by last name. The two volumes for 1812-62 are arranged according to date, so the information obtained from the card record of officers will be useful. Please note that both sets (1808-16 and 1812-62) must be examined since the dates overlap. Data in these records include the date of acceptance of a commission and sometimes an oath of allegiance and the place of residence. If you wish to ferret out the last scrap of information on an officer, you may wish to look at two other series, both in Record Group 45: Letters Resigning, and Confirmations of Appointments.

If your suspected Marine ancestor did not appear in the volume by Callahan, he could have been an enlisted man. Two files in the National Archives pertain to enlisted Marines. The first is the Card Index of Enlisted Men. This card file is arranged alphabetically by the first several letters of the last name, then by the given name. The card on a given man shows his date and place of enlistment. The second file to be examined is the Service Records which are arranged by year of enlistment (obtained from the card index of enlisted men), then by the first letter of the surname, then by the exact date of enlistment. The records often contain date, place, and term of enlistment, age, description, occupation, size roll data, and discharge information. Knowing the basic information on your officer or enlisted Marine from the above records, you may want to go further and look into the muster rolls for further details:

_Department of the Navy, MUSTER ROLLS OF THE US MARINE CORPS, 1798-1815, National Archives Microfilm Publication T1118, Washington, DC, 16 rolls, rolls 3-4-5 pertain to the War of 1812, not alphabetized.

7. Prisoner of war records

The National Archives has prisoner of war records during 1812-5 which pertain to both US and British servicemen who were captured. The materials (Record Group 94, Entry 127) include (a) correspondence relating to prisoners, (b) letters and lists of prisoners sent from the US Treasury Department to the US Adjutant General's Office, (c) lists of US prisoners at Halifax, Nova Scotia, Quebec, and the West Indies, and (d) lists of prisoners sent from the US Navy Department to the US Adjutant General's Office. The first two sets of materials (a and b) have card indexes (Record Group 94, Entry 128), the third set (c) consists of names arranged alphabetically under the place with Halifax having two lists, and the last set (d) is unindexed. The records may contain all or some of these items: name, rank, military organization, date and place of capture, and date of release. Again, you may go there personally, or have a researcher do the work for you, or you may request National Archives by mail to look in the indexes for you. The general pattern for these procedures was given in the last paragraph, section 3, of this chapter. Not to be overlooked are these published materials:

__Public Archives of Canada, GENERAL ENTRY BOOK OF AMERI-CAN PRISONERS OF WAR AT QUEBEC, Hartford, CT, 1923, 2 volumes.

__D. E. W. Carr, INDEX TO CERTIFIED COPY OF LIST OF AMERI-CAN PRISONERS OF WAR, 1812-15, AS RECORDED IN GEN-

ERAL ENTRY BOOK, OTTAWA, CANADA, US Daughters of 1812, Washington, DC, 1924.

__T. V. and J. Huntsberry, DARTMOOR WAR OF 1812 PRISON, Genealogical Publishing Co., Baltimore, MD, 1984.

__American State Papers, LISTS OF AMERICAN PRISONERS IN THE WAR OF 1812; ASP003 (Vol 3) 632, 655-58; ASP016 (Vol 1) 358, 343, 346, ASP023 (Vol 1) 572-82, Government Printing Office, Washington, DC.

There are also some readily available prisoner of war records for American seamen who were captured by the British from American war ships. These are microfilm copies of records which are in the Public Record Office in London, England. The records, which are available from the Family History Library through its many local Family History Center branches, are as follows:

__British Public Record Office, RECORDS RELATING TO AMERICAN PRISONERS OF WAR, 1812-15, EP Microform, East Ardsley, Yorkshire, England, 1981, 11 reels. Available at Family History Library, Microfilm Numbers 1454583-93, Family History Library, Salt Lake City, UT. Gives name, rank, ship from which captured, date of capture, place of capture, place of birth, age, some details of description, discharge, escape, or death.

There is an excellent published guide to these records which will assist you in their use:

__GUIDE TO RECORDS RELATING TO AMERICAN PRISONERS OF WAR, 1812-15, EP Microform, East Ardsley, Yorkshire, England, 1981.

8. Other National Archives records

The major indexed and alphabetized service records for the Volunteer Army, Regular Army, Navy, and Marine Corps in the War of 1812 have been discussed in the previous six sections. However, these are by no means all of the records. There are many more in the National Archives. Even though they are mostly not indexed, data can often be discovered in them with moderate-length research efforts. Included among these further records are prisoner of war records, privateer records, muster rolls, military post records, orderly and company books, inspection returns, Naval rosters and registers, Marine rosters and registers, desertion lists, medical records, deaths, ship logs, and cartographic records. These are described in the following reference volumes:

_National Archives Staff, GUIDE TO GENEALOGICAL RESEARCH IN THE NATIONAL ARCHIVES, National Archives, Washington, DC, 1982.

_National Archives and Records Service, GUIDE TO THE NATIONAL ARCHIVES OF THE US, The Service, Washington, DC, 1974, see index for War of 1812 entries.

_L. H. Pendell and E. Bethel, PRELIMINARY INVENTORY OF THE RECORDS OF THE ADJUTANT GENERAL'S OFFICE, National Archives Publication PI17, Washington, DC, 1949.

_M. Johnson, RECORDS OF THE US MARINE CORPS, National Archives Inventory 2, Washington, DC, 1970.

_V. E. Baugh, PRELIMINARY INVENTORY OF THE RECORDS OF THE BUREAU OF NAVAL PERSONNEL, National Archives Publication PI123, Washington, DC, 1960.

9. State Archive records

Even though the major source of service records for participants in the War of 1812 is the National Archives, you must not overlook the archives of the states which were either states or territories during 1812-5. Some of them have records which essentially duplicate the information in the National Archives, but oftimes they also have records which contain other information. These records usually relate to militia which never did become attached to the US forces or to militia activities before they officially became US troops. A letter of inquiry, an SASE, and a $5 check with the payee line left blank should be dispatched to the archives which you suspect might have data on your ancestor. You should explain to the archives people that your check is either to defer their costs (including photo-duplication) or to be given to a researcher to examine the records for you. The State Archives and their addresses are as follows:

_For CT, Records Officer, The Adjutant General's Office, State Armory, 360 Broad St., Hartford, CT 06115.

_For DE, Division of Historical and Cultural Affairs, Hall of Records, Dover, DE 19901.

_For GA, Department of Archives and History, 330 Capitol Ave., SW, Atlanta, GA 30334.

_For IL, Director, Archives-Records Management Division, Office of Secretary of State, Springfield, IL 62706.

_For IN, Archives and Records Management Division Military Records, IN State Library, 140 Senate Ave., Indianapolis, IN 46204.

_For KY, KY Division of Archives, 300 Coffee Tree Rd., Frankfort, KY 40602.

_For LA, Director, LA State Archives and Records Secretary of State, PO Box 4422, Capitol Station, Baton Rouge, LA 70804.

_For MD, Archivist, State of MD, Hall of Records, PO Box 828, Annapolis, MD 21401.

_For MA, War Records Section, Room 100, The Adjutant General's Office, Military Division, 100 Cambridge St., Boston, MA 02202.

_For MI, MI History Division, State Archives, 3405 North Logan St., Lansing, MI 48918.

_For MS, Department of Archives and History, PO Box 571, Jackson, MS 39205.

_For MO, The Adjutant General's Office, 1717 Industrial Dr., Jefferson City, MO 65101.

_For NH, The Adjutant General's Office, State Military Reservation, 1 Airport Rd., Concord, NH 03301.

_For NJ, Archives and History Bureau, NJ State Library, 185 West State St., Trenton, NJ 08625.

_For NY, Bureau of War Records, Division of Military and Naval Affairs, Public Security Bldg., State Campus, Albany, NY 12226.

_For NC, The Search Room, Archives Branch, Division of Archives and History, Department of Cultural Resources, 109 East Jones St., Raleigh, NC 27611.

_For OH, Director, Division of Soldier's Claims (Veterans Affairs), Adjutant General's Department, State House Annex, Columbus, OH 43215.

_For PA, Director, PA Historical and Museum Commission, Archives Bldg., Box 1076, Harrisburg, PA 17108.

_For RI, The Adjutant General's Office, 1050 North Main St., Providence, RI 02903.

_For SC, SC Department of Archives and History, PO Box 11188, Capitol Station, 1430 Senate St., Columbia, SC 29211.

_For TN, Archives Section, TN State Library and Archives, 403 7th Ave., North, Nashville, TN 37319.

_For VT, Director, State Office of Veterans' Affairs, City Hall Bldg., Montpelier, VT 05602.

_For VA, Archives Division, VA State Library, 12th and Capitol Sts., Richmond, VA 23219.

10. Other archival sources

In addition to the state archives, there are also some other archives and combined libraries/archives which have War of 1812 materials. These include muster rolls, pay rolls, rosters, recruiting lists, morning reports, enlistment papers, and other service records. These documents often relate to military units which were raised in the nearby region. In addition, many of these archives have original manuscripts relating to bounties, campaigns, battles, courts-martial, naval activities, prisoners, pensions, regiments, orderly books, and claims. If you are interested in an extensive search for all references to your ancestor and to his military unit, you should contact the archives in the region where he enlisted and in the regions where battles he was engaged in were fought.

It is really quite easy to locate the archives which you should write. The following reference works should be consulted, and good use of their indexes should be made.

_P. M. Hamer, editor, A GUIDE TO ARCHIVES AND MANUSCRIPTS IN THE US, Yale University Press, New Haven, CT, 1961.

_THE NATIONAL UNION CATALOG OF MANUSCRIPT COLLEC-TIONS, Edwards, Ann Arbor, MI, 1959-present, numerous volumes, numerous indexes.

_DIRECTORY OF ARCHIVES AND MANUSCRIPT REPOSITORIES IN THE US, National Historical Publications and Records Commission, Washington, DC, 1978.

_D. E. Clanin, US MANUSCRIPT SOURCES FOR A STUDY OF THE WAR OF 1812, in W. J. Welch and D. C. Skaggs, WAR ON THE GREAT LAKES, Kent State University Press, Kent, OH, 1991, pages 100-127.

When using the indexes, you should look up the topic WAR OF 1812 and then pay careful attention to all listings under that category. As you check out the listings, you will come across those which are pertinent to your ancestor's home area or his battle areas. You can then read the descriptions of the holdings of those archives, and if that sounds good, dispatch them an SASE, a $5 check with the payee line left blank, and a request that they or a searcher survey the manuscripts to see if they might be worth a more detailed search. When you look in the indexes, give careful consideration to the following items listed as subdivisions under the category WAR OF 1812: Bounties, Campaigns, Battles, Military actions, Cavalry, Claims, Courts-martial, Defense, Medical, Military life, Military papers, Military service, Naval affairs, Orderly books, Pay allow-ances, Pensions, Prisoners and Prisons, Recruiting, Regiments, Registers, Societies, Soldiers, Supplies, and Veterans' Organizations.

One further important source of War of 1812 servicemen records are the many genealogical periodicals published by national, state, re-gional, and local genealogical societies. These periodicals often contain War of 1812 materials which have surfaced in various repositories in the areas. Locating these records is facilitated by an excellent index to genealogical journal articles:

_PERSI, PERIODICAL SOURCE INDEX, Allen County Public Library Foundation, Fort Wayne, IN, 1986-. Indexes genealogical periodicals 1847-present. Look under states and counties, then under MILI-TARY.

Chapter 3

POST-WAR BENEFITS

1. The legislation

Just before the War, during the War, and shortly after the War, the US Congress passed a series of laws providing inducements for men to join the armed forces and stay throughout the War or for a long period, relief of those disabled, and for relief of the families of those killed or dying in service. These early public laws may be found in:

_PUBLIC STATUTES AT LARGE OF THE US, Little, Brown, Boston, MA; especially Volume 2, pages 669, 671, 728; and Volume 3, pages 67, 287, 332.

The laws provided that (a) every non–commissioned officer, soldier, seaman, or marine would receive 160 acres of land upon his honorable discharge from the service, (b) the heirs [wife, children] of those killed or dying in service would receive 160 acres of land, (c) every soldier, seaman, or marine who was disabled in the service would receive a pension, and (d) heirs of commissioned officers killed in service would receive a pension for 5 years. Late in the war the 160 acres of land was increased to 320 acres for a short period. This land was referred to as bounty land, and it was located in the areas of the IL, MO, and AR Territories.

In 1842, a law was passed permitting qualified veterans to receive bounty land not just in IL, MO, and AR but in any state or territory in which public land was available. As of 1850, commissioned officers were also awarded 160 acres. In 1855, the requirements for bounty land were reduced to 14 days of service or participation in battle action. Then, in 1871 and 1878, two major pension laws were passed. The one of 1871 provided a pension for servicemen who had served 60 days or to widows of such servicemen if they had married before 1815. The law of 1878 provided a pension for servicemen who had served 14 days or participated in a battle, or for their widows. These public laws (of 1842, 1855, 1871, 1878) will be found in:

_PUBLIC STATUTES AT LARGE OF THE US, Little, Brown, Boston, MA, Volume 5, page 497; Volume 10, page 702; Volume 16, page 411; and Volume 20, page 27.

The two types of post-war veteran's benefits (bounty land and pensions) will be discussed in succeeding sections of this chapter. The records of these benefits are often quite valuable genealogically.

2. Bounty land applications

Veterans of the War of 1812 could apply for a warrant (certificate) giving them the right to land (called bounty land) as a reward for their military service. Heirs (widows, children, and sometimes parents) of those killed or dying in service as well as heirs of servicemen dying after the War, were also often eligible for bounty land. The National Archives has bounty land warrant application records relating to these persons. The records are contained in files, each of which consists of a warrant application, a discharge certificate, the action taken on the application (approval or disapproval), and sometimes some supporting documents. Information included in the files will be some of the following items: name, age, residence, rank, military unit, dates of joining and leaving the service, and a personal description. If the application was approved it will also have on it the Congressional Act under which the bounty land was issued, the number of acres issued, and the warrant number. If the application was not approved, it will have on it a register number.

In order to locate the bounty land warrant application records for a given individual, you need to look in two different places. First, you should have a look at the following microfilm index or a published form of it:

_US Veterans Administration, INDEX TO WAR OF 1812 PENSION APPLICATION FILES, National Archives Microfilm Publication M313, Washington, DC, 102 rolls.

_V. D. White, INDEX TO WAR OF 1812 PENSION FILES, National Historical Publishing Co., Waynesboro, TN, 1989, 3 volumes.

The reason for looking in this pension index is that a sizable number of War of 1812 bounty land applications were placed in the pension record files. Thus, you may very well find your ancestor's bounty land records in the same file with his pension materials. So, if your veteran appears in this index, you can proceed to the pension files for the War of 1812. These files with the contents arranged alphabetically are in the National Archives.

_WAR OF 1812 PENSION APPLICATION FILES (Record Group 15), National Archives, Washington, DC, alphabetically arranged.

If you do not locate your ancestor's bounty land application in the above search, you should seek him in the following file:

_POST-REVOLUTIONARY WAR SERIES OF BOUNTY LAND AP- PLICATIONS (Record Group 15), National Archives, Washington, DC, alphabetically arranged.

This is a large set of alphabetically arranged bounty land application files for military service given during the years 1790-1855, which included the War of 1812 dates of 1812-5. Since they are arranged alphabetically, they can be directly searched for your forebear's file.

You may examine the above index and request materials from the files personally at the National Archives; you may hire a researcher to do the work for you; or you may write the National Archives. The procedure has been discussed in the last paragraph, section 3, Chapter 2. In any case, be very careful to record the Congressional Act under which the land was issued, the number of acres, and the warrant number.

3. Bounty land warrants

Once a veteran or his heir had applied for bounty land and had the application approved, a warrant (certificate) entitling him or her to the property was issued. Up until 1842, the land had to be located in specified areas in AR, IL, and MO, but after 1842, any government land could be received. Also, up to 1852, the warrants could not be sold or otherwise transferred to other persons, but after 1852, this could be done. Quite often, however, the regulations were circumvented by having the veteran sign a power of attorney. The records of the transfer of land are in two places: (1) on a set of 14 rolls of microfilm, and (2) in files which are located in the General Archives Division of the National Archives. In general, these records carry little of genealogical value, especially since many of the warrants were sold to other people. This means that the person who originally obtained the warrant and the individual who cashed in the warrant and took up the land were different.

The first place to look is in a set of microfilms which is a reproduction of 105 volumes of bounty land warrants issued 1812-58 to servicemen of the War of 1812 plus four volumes of indexes:
_US Bureau of Land Management, WAR OF 1812 MILITARY BOUNTY LAND WARRANTS, 1815-58, National Archives Microfilm Publication M848, Washington, DC, 14 rolls, with 4 indexes on the first roll.
The first roll contains 4 indexes, rolls 1-13 list 160 acre warrants with numbers 1-28085, and the 14th roll lists 320-acre warrants with numbers 1-1076. The four indexes which are in the 1st roll are: (a) index of MO patentees, (b) index of AR patentees, (c) index of IL patentees with surnames beginning with C or D, and (d) index of patentees under the Act of 1842. The partial IL index is supplemented by a published index:
_US House of Representatives, NAMES OF VETERANS TO WHOM PATENTS WERE ISSUED FOR LAND IN IL FOR SERVICE IN THE WAR OF 1812, House Document 262, 26th Congress, 1st Session, US Government Printing Office, Washington, DC, 1840; reprint edition accompanied by index compiled by L. M. Volkel, Heritage House, Thomson, IL, 1977.

The second place to seek out bounty land warrant records is in the General Archives Division, National Archives and Records Service, Washington Records Center, 4205 Suitland Rd., Suitland, MD 20409. In their records are the following files:

_DOUBLE BOUNTY WARRANTS ISSUED UNDER THE ACT OF MAY 6, 1812, 320 acre warrants 1-1101 (Record Group 49, Entry 13).

_WARRANTS ISSUED UNDER ACTS OF DEC 24, 1811, JAN 11, 1812, MAY 6, 1812, AND JUL 27, 1842, 160 acre warrants 1-28085 (Record Group 49, Entry 14).

_WARRANTS ISSUED UNDER ACT OF FEB 11, 1847, 40 acre warrants 1-7585, 160 acre warrants 1-80689 (Record Group 49, Entry 15).

_WARRANTS ISSUED UNDER ACT OF SEP 28, 1850, 40 acre warrants 1-103978, 80 acre warrants 1-57718, 160 acre warrants 1-27450 (Record Group 49, Entry 16).

_WARRANTS ISSUED UNDER ACT OF MAR 22, 1852, 40 acre warrants 1-9070, 80 acre warrants 1-1699, 160 acre warrants 1-1223 (Record Group 49, Entry 17).

_WARRANTS ISSUED UNDER ACT OF MAR 3, 1855, 10 acre warrants 1-4, 40 acre warrants 1-542, 60 acre warrants 1-359, 80 acre warrants 2-49491, 100 acre warrants 1-6, 120 acre warrants 1-97096, 160 acre warrants 1-115783 (Record Group 49, Entry 18).

In order to obtain a given warrant file from these groups of records, it is necessary to know the Congressional Act under which the warrant was issued, the number of acres, and the warrant number. You will have obtained these three items from your search for the bounty land application as described in the previous section (section 2, Chapter 3). The warrant file contains documents relating to warrant redemption and the land transfer. You need to remember that it may contain essentially no further information on your ancestor, particularly if the warrant had been sold to someone else, as was often the case.

You may look at the microfilms at the National Archives and request the warrant file at the General Archives Division in person; or you may hire a researcher to do these things for you; or you may write the National Archives (PA Ave., between 7th and 9th Sts., Washington, DC 20408) and the General Archives Division (4205 Suitland Rd., Suitland, MD 20409.).

---

4. Pension applications

As mentioned in the first section of this chapter, pensions for War of 1812 participants and their heirs were issued before 1871 only to disabled veterans and to heirs of commissioned officers. In 1871 a law was passed which provided for a pension to be given to all veterans who had served 60 days or to their widows, if the widows had married them before 1815. Another law of 1878 reduced the service requirement to 14 days or involvement in a military engagement. As you can imagine, there were not too many veterans alive in 1871. A youngster of 17 enlisting in 1814 would be 74 years old in 1871! Wives tended to be younger than the veterans, so there was a considerable number of widows.

The pension application files for <u>volunteers</u> in the National Archives are indexed in a microfilm publication and in a published set of volumes:

_US Veterans Administration, INDEX TO WAR OF 1812 PENSION APPLICATION FILES, National Archives Microfilm Publication M313, Washington, DC, 102 rolls.

_V. D. White, INDEX TO WAR OF 1812 PENSION FILES, National Historical Publishing Co., Waynesboro, TN, 1989, 3 volumes.

This is the same index used in seeking bounty land applications (because some bounty land applications were filed in with pension applications). Once you locate an ancestor in this index, you can then go directly to his or her alphabetically arranged pension application file. This file, which is in the National Archives, usually contains the application, a summary of the veteran's service record, and a record of the approval or rejection of the application, and data on the marriage (if it is a widow's application). In these documents, you will generally find the age and residence of the serviceman, his rank, his military units, the date of entrance and release from the service, and other data if it is a widow's application (official who performed the marriage, date and place of veteran's death).

There is also a remarried widow's card index which covers the dates 1812–60, this including War of 1812 related references. This index is alphabetically arranged according to the new remarried name of the veteran's widow. The card shows the pension file number and the name of her former veteran husband. His name will permit you to find his or her pension application papers.

The pension application files for <u>regular army</u>, <u>navy</u>, and <u>marines</u> are indexed in the following:

_US Veteran's Administration, OLD WAR INDEX TO PENSION FILES, National Archives Publication T316, Washington, DC, 7 rolls.

_V. D. White, INDEX TO OLD WARS PENSION FILES, National Historical Publishing Co., Waynesboro, TN, 1987.

This index will lead you to the alphabetically-arranged Old Wars Pension Application Files. There is also an alphabetical file called the YI Series which pertains to naval and marine veterans in the years 1815–37.

---

5. Pension payment records

Once the pension application of a veteran or heir of a veteran of the War of 1812 had been approved, pension payments began, usually on a semi-annual basis. This meant that a large number of payment records were kept. The major series of records of these payments consist of those paid by the Pension Office and those paid by the Treasury Department. The records, which are in the National Archives, are (1) a Pension Office record book of payments to invalid pensioners, 1801–15, (2) 23 Treasury Department record books of payments made 1819–71, (3) Treasury Department final payment vouchers made to Army pensioners in 1819–64, (4) 3 Treasury Department record books of payments made to naval and privateer pensioners, one volume for 1815–38, the second 1838–63, the third 1846–73 [but chiefly 1848–66], (5) Treasury Department final payment vouchers to naval and privateer pensioners, 1815–94, and (6) Pension Office field record books of payments to pensioners, 1805–1912.

Not too many War of 1812 veterans will be found in the first four series (1, 2, 3, and 4 above), and not many more in the fifth series (5 above), because sizable numbers of War of 1812 pensions were not paid until after the passage of relevant laws in 1871 and 1878. Hence, the first and most likely place to look is in the sixth (6) series listed above, namely, the Pension Office field record books of payments to pensioners in 1805–1912. These books are indexed in a set of cards arranged alphabetically by the name of the city where the pension agency paying the pensioner was located. The name of this city can be obtained from the Pension application record of the pensioner (see previous section). Other data which you need from the pension application record in order to locate references in these payment records are: the pension certificate number and the date of the latest Congressional law under which the pension was being paid. You may go to the National Archives yourself to examine these records or you may hire a researcher to do the work, or you may write. See the last paragraph, section 3, Chapter 2, for the general procedure and for suggestions.

If you know your veteran to have received a pension, and you do not turn him or his heir up in these 1805–1912 records, then you should try the other series mentioned above. Instructions are given in:
_National Archives Staff, GUIDE TO GENEALOGICAL RESEARCH IN THE NATIONAL ARCHIVES, The Archives, Washington, DC, 1982, pp. 128–130.
Again for this task, you may do it personally, hire a researcher, or write.

Among the items you may find in these pension payment records are: name of veteran, name of widow, rank of veteran, record of each payment, name of agency through which pension was paid, county or post office address of pensioner, moves of pensioner to other places, date and place of death of pensioner, and names of heirs of pensioner. You must not expect to find all of these, but you have a good chance of finding several.

---

6. Other archival records

The major sources of bounty land records and pension records have been discussed in this chapter, but there are other such records in the collection of the National Archives. These other research resources are not as well cataloged and indexed as are those mentioned above, in fact, many are not indexed at all. However, if you or your hired researcher care to make the time-consuming effort, other data may often be found. To locate these other sources, take a look in:

_National Archives and Records Service, GUIDE TO THE NATIONAL ARCHIVES OF THE US, The Service, Washington, DC, 1974, see these heading in the index: bounty lands, pensions, and War of 1812.

_National Archives Staff, GUIDE TO GENEALOGICAL RESEARCH IN THE NATIONAL ARCHIVES, The Archives, Washington, DC, 1982, pp. 123-139.

_T. M. Boardman, M. R. Trever, and L. W. Southwick, PRELIMINARY INVENTORY OF THE ADMINISTRATIVE RECORDS OF THE BUREAU OF PENSIONS AND THE PENSION SERVICE, National Archives Publication PI55, Washington, DC, 1953.

Further, you must not fail to check for holdings in the various state archives and in other archives. The procedures for these investigations have been given in Chapter 2, sections 9 and 10.

Chapter 4

PUBLICATIONS

1. Introduction

Even during the War of 1812, publications relating to the conflict began to be issued by various governmental, academic, and private agencies. This activity has continued to the present day with numerous volumes and articles being available. Most important to genealogical researchers are rosters, rolls, and registers (listings of servicemen in various military units and groups), battle histories (carrying detailed descriptions of engagements in which your ancestor may have been involved), histories of military units and their activities, state histories (which carry detailed information on the state's participation in the War), and writings by and about military men (both officers and enlisted personnel). The following sections deal with these.

2. Rosters, rolls, and registers

Quite a number of records of the War of 1812 have been copied and published. Included are many registers, rolls, rosters, lists, accounts, and reports which tabulate numerous participants in the conflict. Most of these materials are available in book form, but a few are available as microfilms. Among those which are national in scope are:

_US Congress, DIGESTED SUMMARY OF PRIVATE CLAIMS PRESENTED TO THE HOUSE OF REPRESENTATIVES, 1789-1851, Genealogical Publishing Co., Baltimore, MD, 1970 (1853), 3 volumes. [Includes many War of 1812 claims]
_E. S. Galvin, ANCESTOR INDEX OF THE NATIONAL SOCIETY, US DAUGHTERS OF 1812, Volume 1, 1892-1970, The Society, Washington, DC, 1970.
_P. S. Trolinger, ANCESTOR INDEX OF THE NATIONAL SOCIETY, US DAUGHTERS OF 1812, Volume 2, 1970-92, The Author, Miami, OK, 1993.
_F. I. Ordway, Jr., REGISTER OF THE GENERAL SOCIETY OF THE WAR OF 1812, The Society, Washington, DC, 1972.
_General Society of the War of 1812, THE ROSTER, The Society, Mendenhall, PA, 1989.
_C. S. Peterson, KNOWN MILITARY DEAD DURING THE WAR OF 1812, The Author, Baltimore, MD, 1955.
_D. E. W. Carr, INDEX TO CERTIFIED COPY OF LIST OF AMERICAN PRISONERS OF WAR, 1812-5, GENERAL ENTRY BOOK, OTTAWA, CANADA, National Society, US Daughters of 1812, Washington, DC, 1924.

_US Pension Bureau, LIST OF PENSIONERS ON THE ROLL, 1883, Genealogical Publishing Co., Baltimore, MD, 1970 (1883).

_W. H. Powell, LIST OF OFFICERS OF THE ARMY OF THE US FROM 1779-1900, Gale Research Co., Detroit, MI, 1967 (1900).

_T. H. S. Hamersly, GENERAL REGISTER OF THE US NAVY AND MARINE CORPS, 1782-1882, Hamersly, Washington, DC, 1882. [Officers, including volunteer officers]

In addition to the national sources listed above, there are many pertinent publications relating to individual states. Some of the more important ones of these are:

_For CT: CT Adjutant General's Office, RECORD OF SERVICE OF CT MEN IN THE WAR OF THE REVOLUTION, THE WAR OF 1812, AND THE MEXICAN WAR, The Office, Hartford, CT, 1889; Mrs. C. W. Crankshaw, AN INDEX TO VETERANS OF CT DURING THE WAR OF 1812, The Author, Hartford, Ct, 1964, 2 volumes.

_For DE: DE Public Archives Commission, DE ARCHIVES, AMS Press, New York, NY, 1974 (1911-9), volumes 4-5.

_For GA: GA State Archives, MILITARY COMMISSIONS OF THE STATE OF GA, 1798-1860, The Archives, Atlanta, GA; J. F. Smith, THE CHEROKEE LAND LOTTERY OF GA, 1832, Genealogical Publishing Co., Baltimore, MD, 1969 (1838), [Includes War of 1812 veterans, widows, orphans].

_For KY: G. G. Clift, NOTES ON KY VETERANS OF THE WAR OF 1812, Borderl and Books, Anchorage, KY, 1964; G. G. Clift, REMEMBER THE RAISIN! KY AND KENTUCKIANS AT FRENCHTOWN, KY Historical Society, Frankfort, KY, 1961 [Regiments and lists]; KY Adjutant General's Office, KY SOLDIERS OF THE WAR OF 1812, Genealogical Publishing Co., Baltimore, MD, 1969 (1931), [Over 20000 soldiers]; KY Adjutant General's Office, INDEX TO VETERANS OF AMERICAN WARS FROM KY, KY Historical Society, Frankfort, KY, 1966, microfilm rolls 1-4; Z. F. Smith, THE BATTLE OF NEW ORLEANS, Morton, Louisville, KY, 1904 [list of KY soldiers]; B. H. Young, THE BATTLE OF THE THAMES, Morton, Louisville, KY, 1903 [lists of KY soldiers at the Thames, at Battle of Lake Erie, and other places].

_For LA: P. A. Casey, LA IN THE WAR OF 1812, The Author, Baton Rouge, LA, 1963; M. J. B. Pierson, LA SOLDIERS IN THE WAR OF 1812, LA Genealogical and Historical Society, Baton Rouge, LA, 1963, [Over 15000 names]; LA Adjutant General's Office, THE COMPILED SERVICE RECORDS OF LOUISIANANS IN THE WAR OF 1812, The Office, Baton Rouge, LA.

_For MD: W. M. Marine, THE BRITISH INVASION OF MD, 1812-5, Gale Research Co., Detroit, MI, 1965 (1913), [11000 participants]; F. E. Wright, MD MILITIA, WAR OF 1812, Family Line, Silver Spring, MD, 1979-80, 4 volumes; CITIZEN SOLDIERS AT NORTH POINT

AND FORT McHENRY, SEPTEMBER 12–13, 1814, Charles Saffell, Baltimore, MD, undated; T. V. and J. Huntsberry, MD WAR OF 1812 PRIVATEERS, Mart, 'Baltimore, MD, 1983; T. V. and J. Huntsberry, NORTH POINT IN THE WAR OF 1812, J. Mart, Baltimore, MD, 1985.

_For MA (including ME): J. Barker, RECORDS OF THE MA VOLUN-TEER MILITIA DURING THE WAR OF 1812-4, MA Adjutant General's Office, Boston, MA, 1913 [Includes present- day ME, long list of servicemen]; ME State Archives, VETERANS' CEMETERY RECORDS, Photographic Services Corp., 1975, 15 rolls of microfilm especially roll 11; MA Adjutant General's Office, RECORDS OF MA VOLUNTEER MILITIA CALLED OUT BY THE GOVERNOR TO SUPPRESS A THREATENED INVASION DURING THE WAR OF 1812, Wright and Potter, Boston, MA, 1913.

_For NH: C. E. Potter, MILITARY HISTORY OF THE STATE OF NH, 1623–1861, Genealogical Publishing Co., Baltimore, MD, 1972 (1866); NH Veterans' Council, CEMETERY RECORDS OF NH VETERANS, VOLUME 1; FRENCH AND INDIAN WARS AND WAR OF 1812, The Council, Concord, NH, no date.

_For NJ: NJ Adjutant General's Office, RECORDS OF OFFICERS AND MEN OF NJ IN WARS 1791-1815, Genealogical Publishing Co., Baltimore, MD, 1970 (1909), [More than 10000 names]; NJ State Library, NJ IN THE WAR OF 1812, The Library, Trenton, NJ, Books 1–52, with index, also on 16 rolls of microfilm; NJ State Library, NJ PENSIONERS, WAR OF 1812, The Library, Trenton, NJ, also a few copies on microfilm; R. V. Jackson and G. R. Teeples, INDEX TO MILITARY MEN OF NJ, 1775–1815, Accelerated Indexing Systems, Bountiful, UT, 1977.

_For NY: NY Adjutant General's Office, INDEX OF AWARDS ON CLAIMS OF THE SOLDIERS OF THE WAR OF 1812, Genealogical Publishing Co., Baltimore, MD, 1969 (1860), [More than 17000 claims].

_For NC: NC Adjutant General's Office, MUSTER ROLLS OF THE SOLDIERS DETACHED FROM THE MILITIA OF NC IN 1812 AND 1814, Genealogical Publishing Co., Baltimore, MD, 1980 (1851), [Over 12000 names].

_For OH: OH Adjutant General's Office, ROSTER OF OH SOLDIERS IN THE WAR OF 1812, Genealogical Publishing Co., Baltimore, MD, 1968 (1916), [over 27,000 listings] with G. Garner, INDEX TO ROS-TER OF OH SOLDIERS IN THE WAR OF 1812, Eastern WA Genealogical Society, Spokane, WA, 1974; OH National Society of US Daughters of 1812, INDEX TO GRAVE RECORDS OF THE WAR OF 1812, The Society, Columbus, OH, 1969; Mrs. H. B. Diefenbach, INDEX TO THE GRAVE RECORDS OF SOLDIERS OF THE WAR OF 1812 BURIED IN OH, The Author, Columbus, OH, 1945.

_For PA: J. B. Linn and W. H. Egle, MUSTER ROLLS OF PA VOLUN-TEERS IN THE WAR OF 1812, Genealogical Publishing Co., Baltimore, MD, 1967 (1890), [About 15000 listings], taken from PA ARCHIVES, Series 2, Volume 12, Harrisburg, PA, 1890; PA VOLUNTEERS, WAR OF 1812-4, PA ARCHIVES, Series 6, Volumes 7-10, Harrisburg, PA 1907.

_For SC: SC Confederate and Relic Room, ROSTER OF THE SC MEN WHO SERVED IN THE WAR OF 1812, Columbia, SC.

_For TN: Mrs. J. T. Moore, RECORD OF COMMISSIONS OF OFFICERS IN THE 1796-1815 TN MILITIA, Genealogical Publishing Co., Baltimore, MD, 1977 (1956); M. H. McCown and I. E. Burns, SOLDIERS OF THE WAR OF 1812 BURIED IN TN, TN Society of the US Daughters of 1812, Johnson City, TN, 1959; B. and S. Sistler, TENNESSEANS IN THE WAR OF 1812, Sistler and Associates, Nashville, TN, 1992.

_For VT: B. N. Clark, A LIST OF (VT) PENSIONERS OF THE WAR OF 1812, Genealogical Publishing Co., Baltimore, MD, 1969 [Limited to Chittenden County]; VT Adjutant and Inspector General's Office, ROSTER OF SOLDIERS IN THE WAR OF 1812-4, Messenger Press, St. Albans, VT, 1933 [15000 names].

_For VA: VA Auditor's Office, MUSTER ROLLS OF THE VA MILITIA IN THE WAR OF 1812, The Office, Richmond, VA, 1852; VA Auditor's Office, PAY ROLLS OF MILITIA ENTITLED TO LAND BOUNTY UNDER THE ACT OF CONGRESS OF 1850, The Office, Richmond, VA, 1851; P. G. Wardell, WAR OF 1812, VA BOUNTY LAND AND PENSION APPLICANTS, Heritage Books, Bowie, MD, 1987.

_For IN Territory: US Adjutant General's Office, MUSTER, PAY, AND RECEIPT ROLLS OF IN TERRITORY VOLUNTEERS OR MILITIA, WAR OF 1812, The Office, Washington, DC, 4 volumes; C. M. Franklin, IN WAR OF 1812 SOLDIERS, Ye Olde Genealogie Shoppe, Indianapolis, IN, 1984.

_For MI: A. T. Miller, SOLDIERS OF THE WAR OF 1812 WHO DIED IN MI, The Author, Ithaca, MI, 1962.

_For IL Territory and IL: H. G. Felty, IL TERRITORY MILITIA, WAR OF 1812, IL Genealogical Quarterly, Volume 5 (Number 3, 1973) 137-143; Volume 8 (Number 4, 1976) 185-88, Volume 9 (Number 1, 1977) 7-14; F. E. Stevens, IL IN THE WAR OF 1812, IL State Historical Society Transactions (1904) 62-197; L. Volkel, WAR OF 1812 BOUNTY LAND PATENTS IN IL, Heritage House, Thomson, IL, 1977 (1840); IL Society of the National Society of the US Daughters of 1812, ALPHABETICAL LIST OF ANCESTORS, The Society, Springfield, IL, 1955; US General Land Office, INDEX TO THE IL MILITARY PATENT BOOK, Woodcock, Peoria, IL, 1853; IL Military and Naval Department, RECORDS OF THE SERVICES OF IL SOLDIERS IN ---<SEVERAL WARS INCLUDING>--- PROTECTING THE FRONTIER FROM THE RAVAGES OF THE INDIANS FROM 1810-13, The Department, Springfield, IL, 1882.

_For <u>MS</u> <u>Territory</u> (MS, AL): MS Department of Archives and History, ROSTER OF MS MEN WHO SERVED IN THE WAR OF 1812 AND THE MEXICAN WAR, The Department, Jackson, MS; E. O. Rowland, MS TERRITORY IN THE WAR OF 1812, Genealogical Publishing Co., Baltimore, MD, 1968 (1921), [7500 soldiers]; P. J. Gandrud, AL REVOLUTIONARY, 1812, AND INDIAN WAR SOLDIERS' SUR- NAMES, McLane, Hot Springs, AR, 1974–, nine volumes.
_For <u>LA</u> <u>Territory</u> (AR, MO, NE, etc.): K. Christensen, AR MILITARY BOUNTY GRANTS, WAR OF 1812, AR Ancestors, Hot Springs, AR, 1971, [6600 names]; NE Secretary of State, ROSTER OF SOLDIERS, SAILORS, AND MARINES OF THE WAR OF 1812, MEXICAN WAR, AND THE WAR OF THE REBELLION RESIDING IN NE, in 1891, in 1893, in 1895, and in 1897, The Secretary, Various publishers, Lincoln, NE, 1892, 1893, 1895, and 1898, 4 volumes.

3. Battle histories

Once you have discovered the various battles in which your ancestor fought, it will be of interest to you to read about each battle in detail. This will permit you to picture him as he was involved in the engagement, and in many cases, you will be able to come up with a general idea of where his unit was in the battle line and how it encountered the enemy. Given below in chronological order are some recommended volumes for the major battles. You need to understand that these are simply suggestions to help get you started in your reading. In each case, there are usually other books which you can locate by using a bibliography which will be mentioned later.
_17 Jul 1812, Fort Michilmackinac: L. P. Kellogg, THE CAPTURE OF MACKINAC IN 1812, State Historical Society of WI, Madison, WI, 1913.
_09 August 1812, Brownstown, MI: J. Dalliba, NARRATIVE OF THE BATTLE OF BROWNSTOWN, Longworth, New York, NY, 1816.
_15 Aug 1812, Fort Dearborn, IL: L. T. Helm, THE FORT DEARBORN MASSACRE, Rand McNally, New York, NY, 1912.
_16 Aug 1812, Detroit, MI: A. B. Vorderstrasse, DETROIT IN THE WAR OF 1812; J. F. Clarke, HULL AND THE SURRENDER OF DETROIT, Ellis, Boston, 1913.
_13 Oct 1812, Queenstown Heights, Ontario: E. A. Cruikshank, THE BATTLE OF QUEENSTOWN HEIGHTS, Tribune Press, Welland, Canada, 1904; S. Van Rensselaer, A NARRATIVE OF THE AFFAIR OF QUEENSTOWN, Leavitt, Lord, & Co., New York, NY, 1856.
_21 Nov 1812, Fort Niagara, NY: E. A. Cruikshank, THE DOCUMENT- ARY HISTORY OF THE CAMPAIGN UPON THE NIAGARA FRONTIER, Tribune Press, Welland, Canada, 1896–1908, 9 volumes.
_17–18 Dec 1812, Mississineway, IN: M. Holliday, THE BATTLE OF MISSISSINEWA, Grant County Historical Society, Marion, IN, 1964.

_18–22 Jan 1813, Frenchtown/River Raisin, MI: G. G. Clift, REMEM-BER THE RAISIN, KY Historical Society, Frankfort, KY, 1961.

_27 Apr 1813, York, Ontario: B. Cumberland, THE BATTLE OF YORK, William Briggs, Toronto, Canada, 1913; M. M. Quaife, THE YAN-KEES CAPTURE YORK, Wayne University Press, Detroit, MI, 1955.

_28 Apr–09 May 1813, Fort Meigs, OH: J. P. Averill, FORT MEIGS, Blade Printing Co., Toledo, OH, 1886.

_27 May 1813, Fort George, Ontario: E. A. Cruikshank, THE BATTLE OF FORT GEORGE, Niagara Historical Society, Niagara, NY, 1904.

_29 May 1813, Sackett's Harbor, NY: O. B. Wilcox, SACKETT'S HARBOR AND THE WAR OF 1812, Jefferson County Historical Society, Watertown, 1886.

_06 Jun 1813, Stoney Creek, Ontario: B. E. Smith, STONEY CREEK, Wentworth Historical Society, Hamilton, Canada, 1925; C. M. Johnson, THE BATTLE FOR THE HEARTLAND: STONEY CREEK, Pennell Press, Stoney Creek, Canada, 1963.

_02 Aug 1813, Fort Stephenson, OH: E. Whittlesey, DEFENSE OF FORT STEPHENSON, Toledo, OH, 1958.

_10 Sep 1813, Americans Capture British Lake Erie Fleet: R. Dillon, WE HAVE MET THE ENEMY, McGraw-Hill, New York, NY, 1978; M. C. Perry, THE BATTLE OF LAKE ERIE, Gray Printing, Fostoria, OH, 1967.

_01 Oct 1813, Fort Mims, AL: F. L. Wosley, THE FORT MIMS MASSACRE, Alabama Review, Volume 24, 1971, pp. 194–204; H. S. Halbert, THE CREEK WAR OF 1813 AND 1814, Donohue & Henneberry, Chicago, IL, 1895.

_05 Oct 1813, Thames River, Ontario: F. C. Hamil, THE VALLEY OF THE LOWER THAMES, University of Toronto Press, Toronto, Canada, 1951.

_26 Oct 1813, Chateaugay, Quebec: W. D. Lighthall, AN ACCOUNT OF THE BATTLE OF CHATEAUGAY, Drysdale & Co., Montreal, Canada, 1899.

_11 Nov 1813, Chrysler's Farm, Ontario: R. Sellar, CHRYSLER, THE DECISIVE BATTLE OF THE WAR OF 1812, Gleaner Office, Huntington, Quebec, 1913.

_19 Dec 1813, Fort Niagara, NY: M. M. Wilner, NIAGARA FRONTIER, Clarke, Chicago, IL, 1931, 3 volumes.

_27 Mar 1814, Horseshoe Bend, AL: H. S. Halbert, THE CREEK WAR OF 1813 AND 1814, Donohue & Henneberry, Chicago, IL, 1895.

_25 Jul 1814, Lundy's Lane, Ontario: AN ACCOUNT OF THE BATTLE OF LUNDY'S LAND, Tribune Press, Welland, Canada, 1888.

_14 Aug 1814, Fort Erie, Ontario: E. A. Cruikshank, THE SIEGE OF FORT ERIE, Lundy's Lane Historical Society, Lundy's Lane, Canada, 1905.

_24 Aug 1814, Bladensburg, MD: US Infantry School, THE BATTLE OF BLADENSBURG, Infantry School Press, Camp Bennington, 1921.

_06-11 Sep 1814, Plattsburg, NY: A. S. Everest, RECOLLECTIONS OF CLINTON COUNTY AND THE BATTLE OF PLATTSBURG, Clinton County Historical Society, Plattsburg, NY, 1964.
_11 Sep 1814, Americans Take British Fleet on Lake Champlain: C. G. Muller, THE PROUDEST DAY: MACDONOUGH OF LAKE CHAMPLAIN AND LAKE GEORGE, Bobbs-Merrill, Indianapolis, IN, 1946.
_13 Sep 1814, Fort McHenry, MD: FORT MCHENRY, Green Lucas, Baltimore, MD, 1921; H. I. Lessem, FORT MCHENRY NATIONAL MONUMENT, National Park Service, Washington, DC, 1950; J. C. Linthicum, THE PART PLAYED BY FORT MCHENRY IN OUR SECOND WAR WITH ENGLAND, Government Printing Office, Washington, DC, 1912.
_01-09 Jan 1815, New Orleans, LA: R. Reilly, THE BRITISH AT THE GATES: THE NEW ORLEANS CAMPAIGN, Putnam, New York, NY, 1974.

It may be that your ancestor served in the naval forces and that you wish to read further regarding some of the sea or lake battles in which he participated. Among the major encounters and books which are recommended for your use are:
_19 Aug 1812, USS Constitution over HMS Guerriere: B. Grant, EAGLE OF THE SEAS: THE STORY OF OLD IRONSIDES, Rand McNally, Chicago, IL, 1949; T. P. Morgan, OLD IRONSIDES, THE STORY OF THE USS CONSTITUTION, Burdette, Boston, MA, 1963; J. Jennings, TATTERED ENSIGN, THE STORY OF AMERICA'S MOST FAMOUS FIGHTING SHIP, USS CONSTITUTION, Crowell, New York, NY, 1966.
_18 Oct 1812, USS Wasp over HMS Frolic: B. F. Stevens, THE WASP AND THE FROLIC AND OTHER INCIDENTS OF THE WAR OF 1812, United Services, Volume 42, 1905, pp. 181-9.
_25 Oct 1812, USS United States over HMS Macedonian: WE MUST FIGHT HER; THE UNITED STATES VS. THE MACEDONIAN, US Naval Institute Proceedings, Volume 99, 1973, pp. 90-3.
_29 Dec 1812, USS Constitution over HMS Java: J. R. Soley, THE FIGHT BETWEEN THE CONSTITUTION AND THE JAVA, Military Historical Society of Massachusetts Papers, Volume 11, 1901, pp. 121-40, also references under 19 Aug 1812.
_24 Feb 1813, USS Hornet over HMS Peacock: R. W. Neeser, HISTORIC SHIPS OF THE NAVY - HORNET, US Naval Institute Proceedings, Volume 67, 1941, 218-51.
_01 Jun 1813, HMS Shannon over USS Chesapeake: K. Poolman, GUNS OFF CAPE ANN, THE STORY OF THE SHANNON AND THE CHESAPEAKE, Rand McNally, Chicago, IL, 1961; C. B. Crosby, THE CHESAPEAKE, A BIOGRAPHY OF A SHIP, Norfolk National Society, Norfolk, VA, 1968.

_14 Aug 1813, HMS Pelican over USS Argus: J. Inderwick, CRUISE OF THE USS BRIG ARGUS IN 1813, New York Public Library, New York, NY, 1917.

_05 Sep 1813, USS Enterprise over HMS Boxer: S. Pickering, SEAFIGHT OFF MONHEGAN, ENTERPRISE AND BOXER, Machigonne, Portland, ME, 1941.

_10 Sep 1813, Americans capture British Lake Erie Fleet: R. Dillon, WE HAVE MET THE ENEMY, McGraw-Hill, New York, NY, 1978; R. J. Dodge, THE BATTLE OF LAKE ERIE, Gray Printing, Fostoria, OH, 1967.

_28 Mar 1814, HMS Phoebe and Cherub over USS Essex: F. Donovan, THE ODYSSEY OF THE ESSEX, McKay, New York, NY, 1969.

_28 Jun 1814, USS Wasp over HMS Reindeer: L. Hunt, OUR LAST YARDARM FIGHT, THE WASP AND THE REINDEER, Harvard Graduate Magazine, Volume 37, 1929, pp. 418-28.

_07 Sep 1814, USS Wasp over HMS Avon: A. Farcholt, USS WASP, US Naval Institute Proceedings, Volume 70, 1944, pp. 190-2.

_11 Sep 1814, Americans take British Fleet on Lake Champlain: G. G. Muller, THE PROUDEST DAY, MACDONOUGH OF LAKE CHAMPLAIN, John Day, New York, NY, 1960; L. W. Dean, GUNS OVER CHAMPLAIN, Rinehart, New York, NY, 1946; F. F. Van de Water, LAKE CHAMPLAIN AND LAKE GEORGE, Bobbs-Merrill, Indianapolis, IN, 1946.

_14 Jan 1815, HMS Endymion, Tenados, and Pomone over USS President: M. C. Perry, REMARKS OF THE USS PRESIDENT, US Naval Institute Proceedings, Volume 15, 1889, pp. 339-46.

_20 Feb 1815, USS Constitution over HMS Cyane and Levant: C. W. Fisher, THE LOG OF THE CONSTITUTION, FEB 21-4, 1815, THE CAPTURE OF THE CYANE AND THE LEVANT, US Naval Institute Proceedings, Volume 43, 1917, pp. 22732, also references under 19 Aug 1812.

_23 Mar 1815, USS Hornet over HMS Penguin: R. W. Neeser, HISTORIC SHIPS OF THE NAVY - HORNET, US Naval Institute Proceedings, Volume 67, 1941, pp. 218-41.

_30 Jun 1815, USS Peacock over HMS Nautilus: T. F. Davis, USS PEACOCK IN THE WAR OF 1812, FL Historical Quarterly, Volume 16, 1938, pp. 231-41.

Additional books and articles on the War of 1812, including many materials on the various land and sea battles, are listed in the following bibliographies:

_J. C. Fredricksen, WAR OF 1812 RESOURCE GUIDE, Subia, Los Angeles, CA, 1979.

_D. L. Smith, WARS OF THE US, BIBLIOGRAPHIES, WAR OF 1812, Garland Publishing Co., New York, NY, 1986.

---

4. Unit histories

In addition to the numerous regimental materials which are located in manuscript form in state and other archives (see Chapter 2, Sections 9 and 10), there are some published records of some of these military units. These accounts are best located by looking in the two bibliographies listed above (Fredricksen and Smith) and by looking under US-HISTORY-WAR OF 1812-Regimental histories in larger libraries and catalogs. Libraries in the region of origin of the regiment are obviously preferable. For example, if you are searching for historical material relating to a VT regiment, large libraries in VT will be the places to look. Such libraries for VT (and for other states) will be found listed in:

_V. N. Chambers, editor, THE GENEALOGICAL HELPER, Everton Publishers, Logan, UT, latest May-June issue.

Other large libraries such as the Library of Congress, the New York City Library, and the Newberry Library in Chicago should also be considered.

Another important source of both published and unpublished materials on War of 1812 regiments is:

_The US Army Military History Institute, Carlisle Barracks, PA 17013.

This institute is the Army's official central repository for historical source materials of the US Army. Send them your ancestor's military unit, along with an SASE, and ask them to see what they have regarding his unit. You need to remember that the institute does not trace individuals, but concerns itself only with the histories of the army's units.

Among the very useful regimental histories are the following:

_W. T. Brady, THE TWENTY-SECOND INFANTRY IN THE WAR OF 1812, Western PA Historical Magazine 32 (1949) 56-60; and J. N. Crombie, THE TWENTY-SECOND US INFANTRY, A FORGOTTEN REGIMENT IN A FORGOTTEN WAR, PA Historical Magazine 60 (1967) 133-47, 221-31.

_F. R. Brown, HISTORY OF THE NINTH US INFANTRY, 1799-1909, Donnelley, Chicago, IL, 1919.

_B. Elkannah and T. S. Fiske, A WAR HISTORY OF THE SIXTH US INFANTRY, 1798-1903, Hudson-Kimberly, Kansas City, MO, 1903.

_C. E. Hampton, HISTORY OF THE TWENTY-FIRST US INFANTRY, Miller, Columbus, OH, 1911.

_J. D. Holmes, THE LA INFANTRY REGIMENT AND MILITIA COMPANIES, 1766-1821, The Author, Birmingham, AL, 1965.

_J. H. Niebaum, HISTORY OF THE PITTSBURGH WASHINGTON INFANTRY, 102ND (OLD 13TH) REGIMENT PA, Burgum Printing Co., Pittsburgh, PA, 1931.

_A. C. Quisenberry, KY TROOPS IN THE WAR OF 1812, Register of the KY Historical Society, 10-13 (1912-15), series of articles.

The procedures of the first paragraph may be employed for locating published works on ships, except that the category used for searching card catalogs should be US- HISTORY-WAR OF 1812-Naval operations. Also, take a careful look at the histories of naval battles and ships given in Section 3 of this chapter.

5. State histories

Another approach which often proves to be exceptionally informative is to read about the War of 1812 military activities of the state or territory under which your ancestor served. To locate these volumes, you need to use the following set of books:

_M. J. Kaminkow, US LOCAL HISTORIES IN THE LIBRARY OF CONGRESS, Magna Carta, Baltimore, MD, 1975, 4 volumes and supplement.

Be sure and look up your ancestor's state in the 4 volumes and also in the supplement. Examine all the listings under the heading 1775-1865.

While you are looking in the volumes by Kaminkow, you should also look for general state histories in which sections on the War of 1812 might appear. These will be listed under the heading GENERAL WORKS. HISTORIES.

If you care to really press your investigation to its limits, you can use the appropriate state historical bibliographies. These, too, are to be found listed in the volumes by Kaminkow. They appear at the very beginning of the material on each state under the heading SELECTED BIBLIOGRAPHIES.

Five other categories that you might as well explore when you make your foray into Kaminkow's reference volumes are MUSEUMS, GAZETTEERS, BIOGRAPHY, GENEALOGY, and HISTORIC MONUMENTS. Quite often you will come up with useful materials.

6. Biographies, memoirs, diaries

In the process of obtaining service, bounty land, and pension records on your ancestor, in tracking the exploits of his military unit or ship, and in reading about the campaigns and battles in which he took part, you will have discovered who his officers were. In a number of cases, these officers wrote memoirs, diaries, or other accounts of their military activities. In some instances of officers who later became well-known, they wrote autobiographies and/or biographies of them were written. These works also contain materials on the War of 1812. By locating and reading these works, further insight into your ancestor's times and conditions can be obtained.

Once you know who your ancestor's officers were, you should begin by looking them up in the following volumes. These books give brief summaries of their military careers.

_F. S. Heitman, HISTORICAL REGISTER AND DICTIONARY OF THE US ARMY, US Government Printing Office, Washington, DC, 1903, volume 1.

_E. W. Callahan, LIST OF OFFICERS OF THE NAVY OF THE US AND OF THE MARINE CORPS FROM 1775 TO 1900, Haskell House, New York, NY, 1901.

_WHO WAS WHO IN AMERICAN HISTORY, VOLUME 3: THE MILITARY, Marquis Publications, Chicago, IL, 1975.

Then you can go on to search for published material by or about them. The general procedure is to get into the card catalogs of large libraries, especially those in the officer's state, or near military sites where he was especially active, or near where he lived and/or died after the war. In these card catalogs you should look under the officer's name and under the headings US-HISTORY-WAR OF 1812-Biography and US-HIS-TORY-WAR OF 1812-Personal narratives. A final source of writings by and about officers is to make good use of manuscript holdings in various archives. To locate these data, look under the officer's names in the manuscript finding volumes mentioned in Chapter 2, section 10.

7. Libraries

The final note of importance needs to be sounded in this chapter dealing with publications concerning the War of 1812. Whenever you are near a good, large library (the larger, the better), you should take the occasion to look into their card catalog in hopes of locating further information pertaining to the War of 1812 and your ancestor's part in it. The headings under which you have the best chance of finding relevant publications are as follows: BOUNTIES, MILITARY-US; PENSIONS, MILITARY-US-WAR OF 1812; PENSIONS, MILI-TARY-US-(VARIOUS STATES); US-HISTORY-WAR OF 1812-all subheadings, especially Afro-American troops, American forces, Biography, British forces, Campaigns and battles, Canadian forces, Cartography, Centennial celebrations, Chronology, Claims, Conscien- tious objectors, Destruction and pillage, Foreign participation, Hospitals, Jewish partici-pation, Maps, Medical affairs, Museums, Naval operations, Periodicals, Personal narratives, Pictorial works, Prisoners and prisons, Prizes, Refu-gees, Regimental histories, Registers, lists, etc., Registers of dead, Secret service, Societies, Sources, Women.

Names and locations of libraries with good to excellent War of 1812 collections may be found in:

_M. L. and H. C. Young, DIRECTORY OF SPECIAL LIBRARIES, Gale
   Research Co., Detroit, MI, latest edition.
_L. Ash, SUBJECT COLLECTIONS, Bowker, New York, NY, latest
   edition.
You may locate libraries in cities and towns near the places where your
ancestor took part in military action by using:
_AMERICAN LIBRARY DIRECTORY, Bowker, New York, NY, latest
   edition.
Don't forget to enclose an SASE when you write a library. And please
remember, before travelling to visit any library, be sure and dispatch them
an SASE and an inquiry concerning whether they have records which
might help you and what times they are open.

Chapter 5

LOCAL SOURCES

1. Introduction

In addition to national and state sources of data on War of 1812 personnel, there are likely to be at least some records at the city, town, and/or county levels. Among the possibilities are family Bible records, cemetery records, gravestone inscriptions, church records, city histories, town histories, county histories, court records, genealogical periodical articles, local genealogical societies, local historical societies, marriage anniversary accounts in newspapers, mortuary records, newspaper accounts of battles, newspaper obituaries, and published family genealogies. These and many other possible sources of genealogical information on your War of 1812 ancestor are treated in detail with precise instructions for searching in:

_Geo. K. Schweitzer, GENEALOGICAL SOURCE HANDBOOK, $15 postpaid from Geo. K. Schweitzer, 407 Ascot Court, Knoxville, TN 37923.

In the three sections to follow some of the better possibilities from among the above local sources will be discussed in detail. It is important to check the cities, towns, and counties where your ancestor lived when he enlisted, where he lived after the war, and where he died.

2. Place of enlistment

If you know the city, town, and/or county where your War of 1812 veteran enlisted, there are a number of searches you can make in order to find records. The first inquiry should take place within your family to see if anyone knows of records which were kept in a family Bible or prayer book. The most usual things recorded there were birth, marriage, and death dates, but sometimes War of 1812 enlistments or service were recorded. You should also inquire to see if anyone in the family knows of the existence of a family genealogical account which has been published.

The second approach you should make is to look for city, town, and/or county history books, especially ones published within 60 years after the War of 1812. These often carried details of military units raised in their area along with rosters of men who served from the locality. To find such histories, consult:

_M. J. Kaminkow, US LOCAL HISTORIES IN THE LIBRARY OF CONGRESS, Magna Carta, Baltimore, MD, 1975, 5 volumes. Once you have located pertinent volumes, you may have them borrowed for you through interlibrary loan at your local library.

Then, <u>thirdly</u>, you can dispatch an SASE to the city clerk, the town clerk, and/or the county court clerk to ask if any War of 1812 enlistee, discharge, and/or burial records were kept. The addresses of many of these clerks may be obtained from:

_G. B. Everton, Sr., HANDY BOOK FOR GENEALOGISTS, Everton Publishers, Logan, UT, latest edition.

_E. P. Bentley, COUNTY COURTHOUSE BOOK, Genealogical Publishing Co., Baltimore, MD, latest edition.

As a <u>fourth</u> action to take, letters of inquiry along with SASEs should be addressed to the local genealogical society, the local historical society, and the local library. Your inquiries to the genealogical and historical societies should ask about any War of 1812 records giving enlistees and/or local military unit histories. Addresses of local genealogical societies may be obtained from:

_M. K. Meyer, DIRECTORY OF GENEALOGICAL SOCIETIES IN THE USA, Libra Publications, Pasadena, MD, latest edition.

_J. Konrad, GENEALOGICAL AND HISTORICAL SOCIETIES, Summit Publications, Munroe Falls, OH, latest edition.

_V. N. Chambers, editor, THE GENEALOGICAL HELPER, Everton Publishers, Logan, UT, latest July-August issue.

Addresses of local historical societies will be found in the volume just mentioned by Konrad and in:

_DIRECTORY: HISTORICAL SOCIETIES AND AGENCIES IN THE US AND CANADA, Nashville, TN, latest edition.

Your letter and SASE to the local library should ask about local histories, church records, and newspapers published during and after the war. Addresses of local libraries are obtainable in:

_AMERICAN LIBRARY DIRECTORY, Bowker, New York, NY, latest issue.

A <u>fifth</u> approach that often pans out is another quest for newspaper information. You should see if the following volumes list any local newspapers for the local area of your interest during the war years.

_C. S. Brigham, HISTORY AND BIBLIOGRAPHY OF AMERICAN NEWSPAPERS, 1690-1820, American Antiquarian Society, Worcester, MA, 1961, 2 volumes.

_NEWSPAPERS IN MICROFORM, US, Library of Congress, Washington, DC, latest edition. Many of these may be borrowed.

Should you discover newspapers which appear promising, the volumes above give you information regarding where they may be obtained.

---

3. Place of residence With a knowledge of the city, town, and/or county (or cities, towns, and/or counties) in which your veteran lived after the War, you can pursue your search even further. Again, as a <u>first</u> step, you should make another careful survey of your family to make sure you haven't missed a great aunt or some other of the oldest living members.

Then, in the same fashion as before (section 2), the <u>second</u> approach involves the search for city, town, and/ or county histories for the areas where your ancestor lived. Histories often carried biographical references or even sketches of citizens, and often War of 1812 service will be mentioned, sometimes considerable detail being given. The works by Kaminkow (section 2) should be consulted, and, if you locate suitable volumes, your local library can probably borrow them on interlibrary loan.

The <u>third</u> action to take is the sending of inquiries (including SASEs) to local historical societies, local genealogical societies, and local libraries asking about War of 1812 records, especially (a) newspaper accounts of marriage anniversaries of your veteran, (b) records of War of 1812 organizations to which your ancestor or his descendants may have belonged, and (c) local histories which are available. The procedures for obtaining addresses to which you should write have been explained in section 2, this chapter.

A <u>fourth</u> thing to do is to carry out the search for appropriate newspapers by using the three reference volumes given in paragraph 5, section 1, of this chapter.

4. Place of death

Knowing the place and exact or approximate date of death of your War of 1812 veteran, there are numerous routes of exploration you need to take for information concerning him. <u>First</u>, check with your family concerning the existence of family Bible or prayer book records. It is possible that your ancestor's death date in the record may carry a notation about military service.

<u>Second</u>, address an inquiry accompanied by an SASE and a check for $4 to the caretaker of the cemetery in which your ancestor is buried. Ask if there are any detailed records on those who have been buried there, and if so, whether there is anything about your ancestor's War of 1812 record. If you have not seen the gravestone, also ask for a copy or a picture of the inscription, since these inscriptions often carried notations on military service.

<u>Third</u>, address letters of inquiry accompanied by SASEs to the local library, local genealogical society, and local historical society. Ask them about several things: (a) whether there are local burial or death records

which might mention War of 1812 service, (b) whether existing mortuaries might still have records of previous mortuaries which could have handled the burial, (c) whether there are local church records which might have burial data in them, (d) whether there might be a newspaper obituary, (e) whether there are city, town, or county histories which might give War of 1812 soldier biographies, and (f) whether there might have been a patriotic organization which took part in the funeral service and kept a record of it. Addresses for libraries and societies will be found in the volumes mentioned in section 2 of this chapter.

Fourth, be sure to check the following set of books for local histories which might give War of 1812 veteran data:
_M. J. Kaminkow, US LOCAL HISTORIES IN THE LIBRARY OF CONGRESS, Magna Carta, Baltimore, MD, 1975, 5 volumes.

Finally, don't overlook a newspaper search using the volumes listed in item 5 of section 2 of this chapter.

Chapter 6

SITES, SIGHTS, AND CITES

████████████████ In the process of delving deeper and deeper
1. Introduction into your War of 1812 ancestor's military
████████████████ career, you are likely to accumulate a sizable
amount of information.   Many of these data
may deal with places your forebear was (cities, towns, areas, camp sites,
battle fields, river crossings, rivers, lakes, ports, harbors, trails, routes).
Other data will probably cause you to wonder about the uniforms he wore,
the weapons he used, the equipment he carried, the tents he camped in,
the cities he attacked and/or retreated from, the food he ate, the hospitals
he was treated in, the prisons he was held in, the earthworks from behind
which he fought, and how he and his companions entertained themselves.
There are a number of physical and geographical remains of the War of
1812 which will permit you to gain further insight into your veteran's
military situation.   We will examine historic sites, maps, museums, and
patriotic organizations, all of which can fill you in with regard to the War
of 1812.

████████████████ Some organizations, both governmental and
2. Historic sites private, have identified, marked, preserved,
████████████████ beautified, and/or restored historical sites
associated with the War of 1812.   Much
enjoyment can be had by visiting those with which your forebear was
affiliated.   In conjunction with some of these places there are libraries,
displays, and/or museums. They are usually very valuable, so please don't
overlook them.

Included in these historic sites are parks, battlegrounds, forts,
monuments, earthworks, houses, and displays.   The following list names
some of the more important of these:
_In AL, Horseshoe Bend National Military Park, near Dadesville, AL;
    Fort Mims Site, in vicinity of Tensaw, AL.
_In FL, Fort San Carlos De Barrancas, US Naval Air Station, Pensacola,
    FL.
_In IN, Tippecanoe Battlefield, 7 miles NE of Lafayette, IN.
_In LA, Chalmette National Battlefield Site, 7 miles S of New Orleans,
    LA.
_In MD, Star Spangled Banner Flag House, 844 E. Pratt St., Baltimore,
    MD; Fort McHenry National Monument and Historic Shrine, Locust
    Point, at E end of Fort Ave., Baltimore, MD; Rodgers Bastion in
    Patterson Park, Baltimore, MD.
_In MA, Battleship USS Constitution, Charlestown Navy Yard, Boston,
    MA.

_In MI, Fort Mackinac, Huron Rd., Mackinac Island, MI.
_In NY, Sackets Harbor Battlefield, Sackets Harbor, NY; Old Fort
  Niagara, N of Youngstown, NY on Highway 18; Plattsburgh Site, just E
  of Plattsburgh, NY; Fort Ontario (Oswego), Oswego, NY.
_In OH, Fort Meigs, 1 mile SW of Perryville, OH; War of 1812 Battle
  Site, East Bay Shore Rd., Mineyah-ta-on-the-Bay, OH; Perry's Victory
  and International Peace Memorial, Put-in-Bay, South Bass Island, OH.
_In PA, USS Niagara, State Street at Lake Erie, Erie, PA.
_In TN, Camp Blount Tablets National Memorial, just S of Fayetteville,
  TN.
_In Ontario, Canada, Fort Malden National Historical Park, Amherstburg;
  Old Fort Henry, Kingston; Fort George National Historic Park,
  Niagara-on-the-Lake; Fort York, Toronto.

    Other historical sites may be found listed in the following volumes.
Simply look under the states and places where your War of 1812 veteran
was during the conflict.
_W. J. Murtagh, NATIONAL REGISTER OF HISTORIC PLACES,
  National Park Service, Washington, DC, 1976, 2 volumes.
_R. M. Ketchum, THE AMERICAN HERITAGE BOOK OF GREAT
  HISTORIC PLACES, American Heritage Publishing Co., New York,
  NY, 1957.

3. Museums

As you continue your War of 1812 research, one of
the best ways to get a feel for the conditions under
which your ancestor fought is to visit some of the
better museums which have collections of materials
from the war. In these museums you will see weapons, uniforms, flags,
insignia, camp furniture, cannons, vehicles, equipment, documents, saddles,
and many other types of relics. Among the most rewarding museums to
pay a visit to are the following:
_In AL, Horseshoe Bend National Military Park, Route 1, Box 3,
  Daviston, AL 36256.
_In IN, Battle Ground Historical Corporation, PO Box 225, Battle
  Ground, IN 47920.
_In LA, Chalmette National Historical Park, St. Bernard Hwy., Chalmette,
  LA 70043.
_In MD, Fort McHenry National Monument and Historic Shrine, Locust
  Point, Baltimore, MD 21230; Star Spangled Banner Flag House, 844 E.
  Pratt St., Baltimore, MD 21202.
_In MA, USS Constitution, Boston National Historical Park, Charlestown,
  Navy Yard, Boston, MA 02129.
_In MI, Detroit Historical Museum, 5401 Woodward Ave., Detroit, MI
  48202; Mackinac Island State Park Commission, PO Box 370, Mack-
  inac Island, MI 49757.

_In NY, Fort Ontario State Historic Site, East 7th St., Oswego, NY 13126; Buffalo and Erie County Historical Society, 25 Nottingham Ct., Buffalo, NY 14216; Pickering-Beach Historical Museum, 503 W. Main St., Sackets Harbor, NY 13685; Sackets Harbor Battlefield State Historic Site, Sackets Harbor, NY 13685; Old Fort Niagara, PO Box 169, Youngstown, NY 14174.
_In PA, Flagship Niagara, Foot of State St., Erie, PA 16507.
_In Ontario, Canada, Fort Malden National Historical Park, Laird Ave., Box 38, Amherstburg, Ontario, Canada N9V 2Z2; The Fairfield Museum, Highway 2, Bothwell, Ontario, Canada NOP, 1CO; Old Fort Henry, Box 213, Kingston, Ontario, Canada K7L 4V8; Lundy's Lane Historical Museum, 5810 Ferry St., Niagara Falls, Ontario, Canada L2G 1S9; Fort George National Historic Park, PO Box 787, Niagara-on-the-Lake, Ontario, Canada L0S 1J0; Fort York, Garrison Rd. at Fleet and Strachan Ave., Toronto, Ontario, Canada M6K 3C3.

Other museums in regions which are pertinent to your ancestor's history may be located by looking under the state, then the place, in:
_THE OFFICIAL MUSEUM DIRECTORY, US, CANADA, The American Association of Museums, Washington, DC, latest edition.

4. Maps

As you make your way through the historical events of your War of 1812 ancestor's life in the military service, it will often help you to visualize certain events (particularly battles, troop movements, and ship journeys) on appropriate maps. You will find some maps in the books on the history of the War as mentioned in section 8 of Chapter 1. In addition, the following may be consulted for detailed maps of specific battle sites and areas:
_UNPUBLISHED GUIDE TO MAPS OF THE WAR OF 1812, In-house Finding Aid, Cartographic Archives Division, National Archives, Washington, DC 20408.

5. Societies

In the years during and following the War of 1812, several organizations dedicated to various means of preserving data on the War and fostering research and publication came into existence. The four largest surviving organizations of this type will be discussed below along with their addresses and membership requirements. You may wish to write them about their work and request membership application materials.

The National Society, US Daughters of 1812, 1461 Rhode Island Ave., NW, Washington, DC 20005 has over 4500 members. Membership is open to female descendants of persons who rendered civil, military, or naval service to the US during the years 1784-1815. Their publications include a quarterly newsletter, a membership roster, and an 1812 ancestors index. They have erected memorial tablets at a number of War of 1812 sites and have contributed to the restoration of the USS Constitution.

The General Society of the War of 1812, PO Box 106, Mendenhall, PA 19357 has a membership of over 1400. To join the society a person must be a male descendant of a veteran of the War of 1812. The society is an amalgamation of four previous groups: The Society of the War of 1812 of MD, The Society of the War of 1812 in PA, New England Association of Soldiers of the War of 1812 (MA), and The Society of the War of 1812 in CT. The group publishes a triennial yearbook, a news-letter, and registers of members and ancestors.

The Star Spangled Banner Flag House, 844 E. Pratt St., Baltimore, MD 21202 is constituted as an organization and has over 800 members. They maintain as a historic site the house in which Mary Pickersgill made the flag that flew over Ft. McHenry when it was under seige in 1814. Adjacent to the house is their War of 1812 museum. They carry out research, maintain a library of over 500 volumes and original papers, and publish newsletter plus several pamphlets. Membership is open to anyone desiring to support their very worthwhile activities.

The Veteran Corps of Artillery, State of NY, and The Military Society of the War of 1812, Seventh Regiment Armory, 643 Park Ave., New York, NY 10021 has a membership of slightly under 300. The society is made up of both hereditary and non-hereditary members, the latter being attached to the Artillery Service Detachment. Hereditary membership entails descent from servicemen ofthe Revolution or the War of 1812, with some restrictions.

Chapter 7

SOURCES FOR BRITISH AND CANADIAN PARTICIPANTS

1. Canadian background

In 1608, the French placed a colony at Port Royal, Nova Scotia, which grew very slowly into a quite sizable French enterprise which was called New France. They expanded southwestward up the St. Lawrence River, so that by 1666, the population was about 3000, and by 1673, about 6700. They soon became active around the Great Lakes, in the area west of the Appalachians behind the English colonies, and down the MS River Valley. In 1670, the English Hudson Bay Company began operating north and west of New France, and the British held Newfoundland, although France also claimed it. As English expansion moved toward and into New France territory, contests over the land led to a series of four wars between the French and the English. These wars were fought in 1689-97, 1702-13, 1744-48, and 1754-63. The second war ended with France ceding Britain Newfoundland, Nova Scotia, and the Hudson Bay areas. The last war, known as the French and Indian War, resulted in the expulsion of France from all its holdings east of the MS River, including what is now the eastern sections of Canada. At this time, there were about 65,000 French settlers in Canada as compared to over a million English in North America.

Britain named most of the Canadian area Quebec after adding some of its land area to Nova Scotia and Newfoundland. In 1774, Quebec was extended southwestward to include what is now Ontario and much of what is now the upper midwestern US. In 1775, the thirteen colonies invited the French Canadians to participate in their rebellion against Great Britain, but the Canadians refused. After the Revolution, over 40,000 US persons who had remained loyal to the British moved into the western parts of Quebec and Nova Scotia. In response to demands of the Loyalists for separate colonies, the western portion of Nova Scotia was made into New Brunswick, and the western portion of Quebec was made into Upper Canada. The large remainder of Quebec was renamed Lower Canada. Figure 7 illustrates the colony boundaries of the Canadian area as of 1812, the year in which Great Britain and the US went to war. As you will recall, the US plan was to take both Upper and Lower Canada, but all their invasion attempts failed.

The Canadian military forces consisted of regiments of British regulars and regiments of Canadians, who were joined by Canadian militia in times of conflict, and sometimes by Indian allies. Canadians often served in the British regiments when they were stationed in the Canadian

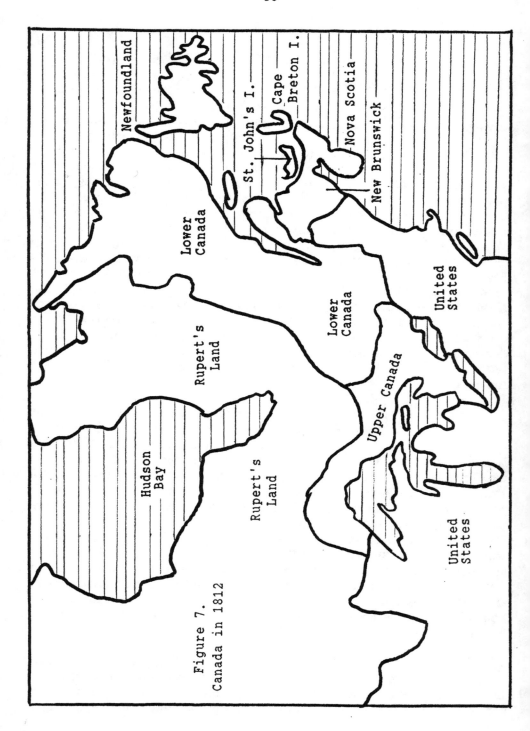

Figure 7.
Canada in 1812

colonies. Following is a list of the British regiments that served in Canada during the War of 1812, along with the battles in which they participated:

__1st ROYAL SCOTS. Fought at Sackett's Harbor (29 May 1813), Fort Niagara (19 Dec 1813), Lewiston (18 Dec 1813), Black Rock (30 Dec 1813), Longwoods (04 Mar 1814), Chippewa (05 Jul 1814), Lundy's Lane 1814), Fort Erie (15 Aug 1814), Cook's Mills (19 Oct 1814).

__3rd EAST KENT. Fought at Plattsburg (11 Sep 1814).

__4th ROYAL LANCASTER. Fought at Bladensburg (24 Aug 1814), Baltimore (13-14 Sep 1814), New Orleans (08 Jan 1815), Fort Bowyer (11 Feb 1815).

__6th ROYAL WARWICKSHIRE. Fought at Fort Erie (15 Aug 1814).

__7th ROYAL FUSILIERS. Fought at New Orleans (08 Jan 1815), Fort Bowyer (11 Feb 1815).

__8th KING'S OWN. Fought at Ogdensburg (22 Feb 1813)), York (27 Apr 1813), Sackett's Harbor (29 May 1813), Stoney Creek (06 Jun 1813), Fort Niagara (19 Dec 1813), Black Rock (30 Dec 1813), Buffalo (30 Dec 1813), Chippewa (05 Jul 1814), Lundy's Lane (25 Jul 1814), Fort Erie (15 Aug 1814), part of them at Plattsburg (11 Sep 1814).

__9th NORFOLK. Fought in no battles.

__13th SOMERSET, LIGHT INFANTRY. Fought at LaColle (30 Mar 1814), Odletown (28 Jun 1814), Plattsburg (11 Sep 1814).

__16th BEDFORDSHIRE. Fought at Plattsburg (11 Sep 1814).

__17th LEICESTERSHIRE. Fought at Plattsburg (11 Sep 1814).

__21st ROYAL SCOTS FUSILIERS. Fought at Bladensburg (24 Aug 1814), Baltimore (13-14 Sep 1814), New Orleans (08 Jan 1815).

__27th ROYAL INNISKILLING. Fought at Plattsburg (11 Sep 1814), New Orleans (08 Jan 1815).

__29th WORCESTERSHIRE. Fought at Fort Castine (01 Sep 1814).

__35th ROYAL SUSSEX. Fought at Plattsburg (11 Sep 1814).

__37th HAMPSHIRE. Fought at Plattsburg (11 Sep 1814).

__39th DORSETSHIRE. Fought at Plattsburg (11 Sep 1814).

__40th PRINCE OF WALES VOLUNTEERS. Fought at New Orleans (08 Jan 1815), Fort Bowyer (11 Feb 1815).

__41st WELSH. Fought at Detroit (16 Aug 1812), Queenston Heights (13 Oct 1812), Frenchtown (22 Jan 1813), Fort Meigs (28 Apr 1813), Fort Stephenson (02 Aug 1813), Fort George (17 Jul 1813), Thames (05 Oct 1813), Stoney Creek (06 Jun 1813),, Chippewa (05 Jul 1814), Lundy's Lane (25 Jul 1814), Fort Erie (15 Aug 1814).

__43rd OXFORDSHIRE. Fought at New Orleans (08 Jan 1815).

__44th ESSEX. Fought at Bladensburg (24 Aug 1814), Baltimore (13-14 Sep 1814), New Orleans (08 Jan 1815), Mobile (11 Feb 1815).

__49th ROYAL BERKSHIRE. Fought at Queenston Heights (13 Oct 1812), York (27 Apr 1813), Fort George (17 Jul 1813), Beaver Dams (24 Jun 1813), Black Rock (30 Dec 1813), Chrysler's Farm (11 Nov 1813), Plattsburg (11 Sep 1814).

__57th WEST MIDDLESEX. Fought in no battles.

__58th RUTLANDSHIRE. Fought at Plattsburg (11 Sep 1814).
__59th SECOND NOTTINGHAMSHIRE. Fought at Plattsburg (11 Sep 1814).
__62nd WILTSHIRE. Fought at Castine (01 Sep 1814).
__70th GLASGOW LOWLAND. Fought in no battles.
__76th WEST RIDING. Fought at Plattsburg (11 Sep 1814).
__81st NORTH LANCASHIRE. Fought at Plattsburg (11 Sep 1814).
__82nd PRINCE OF WALES VOLUNTEERS. Fought at Fort Erie (15 Aug 1814), Cook's Mills (19 Oct 1814).
__85th KING'S SHROPSHIRE LIGHT INFANTRY. Fought at Bladensburg (24 Aug 1814), Baltimore (13-14 Sep 1814), New Orleans (08 Jan 1815).
__88th CONNAUGHT RANGERS. Fought at Plattsburg (11 Sep 1814).
__89th ROYAL IRISH FUSILIERS. Fought at Black Rock (30 Dec 1813), Chrysler's Farm (11 Nov 1813), Fort Niagara (19 Dec 1813), Longwoods (04 Mar 1814), Lundy's Lane (25 Jul 1814), Fort Erie (15 Aug 1814).
__90th PERTHSHIRE. Fought in no battles.
__93rd ARGYLL AND SUTHERLAND HIGHLANDERS. Fought at New Orleans (08 Jan 1815).
__95th DERBYSHIRE. Fought at New Orleans (08 Jan 1815).
__97th QUEEN'S OWN. Fought at Plattsburg (11 Sep 1814).
__100th PRINCE REGENT'S. Fought at Sackett's Harbor (29 May 1813), Fort Niagara (19 Dec 1813), Buffalo (30 Dec 1813), Chippewa (05 Jul 1814), Lundy's Lane (25 Jul 1814), Fort Erie (15 Aug 1814), Cook's Mills (19 Oct 1814).
__102nd ROYAL DUBLIN FUSILIERS. Fought at Bladensburg (24 Aug 1814).
__103rd DUKE OF YORK'S. Fought at Lundy's Lane (25 Jul 1814), Fort Erie (15 Aug 1814), Cook's Mills (19 Oct 1814).

Listed below are Canadian regiments along with marine and foreign regiments. The last two in the list are the foreign regiments and the two just before them are the marine regiments.
__104th NEW BRUNSWICK FENCIBLES. Fought at Sackett's Harbor (29 May 1813), Fort George (17 Jul 1813), Lundy's Lane (25 Jul 1814), Fort Erie (15 Aug 1814), Cook's Mills (19 Oct 1814).
__10th ROYAL VETERAN BATTALION. Fought at Mackinac (17 Jul 1812), Frenchtown (22 Jan 1813).
__ROYAL NEWFOUNDLAND REGIMENT. Fought at Detroit (16 Aug 1812), Frenchtown (22 Jan 1813), Ogdensburg (22 Feb 1813), York (27 Apr 1813), Fort Meigs (28 Apr 1813), Fort George (17 Jul 1813), Sackett's Harbor (29 May 1813), Mackinac (04 Aug 1814).
__CANADIAN FENCIBLE INFANTRY. Fought at Chateaugay (26 Oct 1813), Chrysler's Farm (11 Nov 1813), LaColle (30 Mar 1814), Plattsburg (11 Sep 1814).

__GLENGARRY LIGHT INFANTRY FENCIBLES. Fought at Ogdens-
burg (22 Feb 1813), York (27 Apr 1813), Fort George (17 Jul 1813),
Sackett's Harbor (29 May 1813), Oswego (05 May 1814), Lundy's Lane
(25 Jul 1814), Fort Erie (15 Aug 1814), Cook's Mills (19 Oct 1814).
__1st MARINE BATTALION. Fought at Chrysler's Farm (11 Nov 1813),
LaColle Mill (30 Mar 1814).
__2nd MARINE BATTALION. Fought at Oswego (05 May 1814),
Bladensburg (24 Aug 1814), New Orleans (08 Jan 1815), Fort Bowyer
(11 Feb 1815).
__REGIMENT DE MEURON. Fought at Plattsburg (11 Sep 1814).
__REGIMENT DE WATTEVILLE. Fought at Oswego (05 May 1814),
Fort Erie (15 Aug 1814).

If you are researching a British or Canadian ancestor in the War of
1812, it is best for your background understanding if you have read a
volume or two on the War from the British/Canadian viewpoint. Among
those to be recommended are:
__K. Caffrey, TWILIGHT'S LAST GLEAMING, Stein and Day, New
York, NY, 1977. A British author.
__J. Hannay, HISTORY OF THE WAR OF 1812, BETWEEN GREAT
BRITAIN AND THE USA, Bowes, St. John, New Brunswick, Canada,
1901. A Canadian viewpoint.
__J. M. Hitsman, THE INCREDIBLE WAR OF 1812, University of
Toronto Press, Toronto, Canada, 1965.
__W. Kingsford, THE HISTORY OF CANADA, VOLUME 8, THE WAR
OF 1812, AMS Press, New York, NY, 1895. Excellent detailed history.
__C. P. Lucas, THE CANADIAN WAR OF 1812, Clarendon Press,
Oxford, England, 1906. An account by a strong supporter of Canada.
__W. B. Turner, THE WAR OF 1812, THE WAR THAT BOTH SIDES
WON, Dundurn Press, Toronto, Canada, 1990.
__W. Wood, THE WAR WITH THE US, A CHRONICLE OF 1812,
Brook and Co., Glasgow, Scotland, 1915.

2. Published materials

There are numerous published
materials on the details of the War
of 1812, but not too many listings
and indexes of British and Canadian
participants. The major sources of detailed information on individuals are
archival materials in various repositories in England and Canada. These
archival sources will be dealt with in the next section. In this section, the
published materials will be treated. The most valuable piece of information that you can have before your search is the regiment or ship in which
your ancestor served. With this being known, your investigation will be
greatly facilitated, since the records are generally filed under the regiment
or ship, and there are no overall indexes. If you do not know the regiment or ship, an extensive search for it must be made. The most useful

sources of this information are family records, biographies, censuses, probate records, death records, church records, cemetery records, obituaries, and especially land records, since many veterans applied for military land grants. Should you happen to know or find the name of a battle in which he fought, the listing of regiments in various battles (see the previous section) will narrow your search. Of immense importance to research are two very good bibliographies of the War of 1812, which contain many British and Canadian publications:

__J. C. Fredriksen, FREE TRADE AND SAILORS' RIGHTS, A BIBLI-
OGRAPHY OF THE WAR OF 1812, Greenwood Press, Westport, CT,
1985.
__D. L. Smith, THE WAR OF 1812, AN ANNOTATED BIBLIOGRA-
PHY, Garland Publishing Co., New York, NY, 1985.

These may be consulted to obtain detailed information on various battles, specific ships, and particular campaigns with which your forebear might have been involved.

Some special categories of publications will also likely be pertinent to you, depending upon the degree of understanding of your progenitor that you wish. The first of these are works which deal with the conduct of the War of 1812:

__P. Berton, THE INVASION OF CANADA, 1812–13, Atlantic Monthly
Press, Boston, MA, 1980. Attempted invasions, US failures.
__C. W. Robinson, CANADA AND THE CANADIAN DEFENSE, 1812–
14, Musson Book Co., Toronto, Canada, 1910. Battles, regiments,
militia, Indian allies.
__P. R. N. Katcher, THE AMERICAN WAR, 1812–14, Osprey Publish-
ing Co., Reading, England, 1974. Battles, the armies, militia.
__H. A. Fay, OFFICIAL ACCOUNTS OF ALL THE BATTLES
FOUGHT BETWEEN THE ARMY AND NAVY OF THE US AND
THE ARMY AND NAVY OF GREAT BRITAIN, 1812–15, Conrad,
New York, NY, 1817. Mainly US accounts, but a few British accounts.

A further category of important publications is that of regimental histories of British and Canadian troops:

__C. H. Stewart, THE SERVICES OF BRITISH REGIMENTS IN
CANADA AND NORTH AMERICA, Department of National
Defense, Ottawa, Canada, 1962.
__R. Burgoyne, HISTORICAL RECORDS OF THE 93RD SUTHER-
LAND HIGHLANDERS, Bently, London, England, 1883.
__R. Cannon, HISTORY OF THE KING'S LIVERPOOL REGIMENT,
Harrison, London, England, 1883.
__L. I. Cowper, THE KING'S OWN, THE STORY OF A ROYAL
REGIMENT, Oxford University Press, Oxford, England, 1939.

__C. L. Kingsford, THE STORY OF THE ROYAL WARWICKSHIRE REGIMENT (FORMERLY 6TH FOOT), Offices of Country Life, London, England, 1921.
__R. L. Rogers, HISTORY OF THE LINCOLN AND WELLAND REGIMENT, Industrial Shops for the Deaf, Montreal, Canada, 1954.
__H. H. Walker, A HISTORY OF THE NORTHUMBERLAND FUSILIERS, 1674-1902, Murray, London, England, 1919.
__L. Weaver, THE STORY OF THE ROYAL SCOTS, FORMERLY THE FIRST OR ROYAL REGIMENT OF FOOT, Offices of Country Life, London, England, 1965.
__E. A. Cruikshank, THE GLENGARRY LIGHT INFANTRY, Canadian House, Toronto, Canada, 1920.
__G. W. Nicholson, THE FIGHTING NEWFOUNDLANDERS, A HISTORY OF THE ROYAL NEWFOUNDLAND REGIMENT, Government of Newfoundland, St. Johns, New Brunswick, Canada, 1963.
__J. D. Martin, THE REGIMENT DEWATTEVILLE, Ontario Historical Society Papers and Records, 62 (1960) 17-30.
__G. de Meuron, LE REGIMENT MEURON, 1781-1816, Le Forum Historique, Lausanne, Switzerland, 1983.
__J. Buchan, THE HISTORY OF THE ROYAL SCOTS (21ST) FUSILIERS, 1678-1918, Nelson, London, England, 1924.
__A. C. Whitehouse, THE HISTORY OF THE WELCH (41ST) REGIMENT, Western Mail and Echo, Cardiff, Wales, 1932.
__F. L. Petre, THE ROYAL BERKSHIRE REGIMENT, 49TH/66TH FOOT, The Regiment, Reading, England, 1925.
__L. Butler, THE ANNALS OF THE KING'S ROYAL RIFLE CORPS (85TH), Murray, London, England, 1923, 4 volumes.
__W. A. Squires, THE 104TH REGIMENT OF FOOT, THE NEW BRUNSWICK FENCIBLES, 1803-17, Brunswick, Fredericton, New Brunswick, 1962.

There are also numerous helpful publications having to do with the Canadian militia:
__E. A. Cruikshank, ARTICLES ON THE CANADIAN MILITIA, published in Canadian Military Institute Selected Papers, as follows:
THE ROYAL NEWFOUNDLAND REGIMENT, No. 5 (1893-94) 5-15.
THE GLENGARRY LIGHT INFANTRY, No. 6 (1894-95) 9-23.
THE PROVINCIAL CAVALRY, No. 8 (1896-97) 9-26.
THE INCORPORATED MILITIA, No. 9 70-80.
THE CANADIAN VOLTIGUERS, No. 10 (1899-1900) 9-21.
THE CANADIAN FENCIBLES, No. 11 (1901) 9-22.
THE FRONTIER LIGHT INFANTRY, No. 12 (1902) 9-19.
THE LINCOLN MILITIA, No. 13 (1904) 9-41.
THE MILITIA OF ESSEX AND KENT, No. 14 (1906) 43-60.

THE MILITIA OF NORFOLK, OXFORD, AND MIDDLESEX,
No. 15 (1907) 47–71.
THE YORK MILITIA, No. 16 (1908) 31–54.

The next category pertains to lists of individual participants either in the conflict or related to it:
__E. Jonasson, CANADIAN VETERANS OF THE WAR OF 1812, Wheatfield Press, Winnipeg, Manitoba, Canada, 1981. Veterans on the pension roll as of 1875.
__A. Files and T. M. Rowe, REGISTER OF PERSONS CONNECTED WITH HIGH TREASON, WAR OF 1812–14, Ontario Genealogical Society, Brant County Branch, Brantford, Ontario, Canada, 1985.
__A. Files, MILITIA ROLL, UPPER CANADA GAZETTE, 1826, Ontario Genealogical Society, Brant County Branch, Brantford, Ontario, Canada, 1989. Militia pension list with 1812–15 militia who died or were disabled.
__L. H. Irving, OFFICERS OF THE BRITISH FORCES IN CANADA DURING THE WAR OF 1812–15, Canadian Military Institute, Welland, Ontario, Canada, 1908. Listings taken from land, militia, petition, obituary, and other records.

The last category has to do with documents and records and published finding aids to them:
__W. C. H. Wood, SELECT BRITISH DOCUMENTS OF THE CANADIAN WAR OF 1812, Champlain Society, Toronto, Canada, 1920–28, 4 volumes.
__National Archives of Canada, INDEX TO BRITISH MILITARY RECORDS, C SERIES, 1757–1896, The Archives, Ottawa, Canada, Record Group 8.
__C. A. Christy, MILITARY SOURCES IN THE PUBLIC ARCHIVES OF CANADA, Families 16, No. 4 (1977) 225–241.
__R. G. Gordon and E. G. Maurice, UNION LIST OF MANUSCRIPTS IN CANADIAN REPOSITORIES, Public Archives of Canada, Ottawa, Ontario, Canada, 1975, 2 volumes. Refers to some Canadian militia lists.
__E. A. Cruikshank, INVENTORY OF MILITARY DOCUMENTS IN CANADIAN ARCHIVES, Government Printing Office, Ottawa, Ontario, Canada, 1910.
__R. Higham, A GUIDE TO SOURCES OF BRITISH MILITARY HISTORY, University of CA Press, Los Angeles, CA, 1971.
__E. and E. Sykes, SUPPLEMENTARY INDEX TO CANADIAN RECORDS, Genealogy Department, Salt Lake City, UT, 1985, 3 volumes. Index to genealogical articles. References to militia lists in various places, both in archives and as published works.
The last five reference sources will be of considerable value to you as you seek archival records in accordance with the next section.

3. Archival records

There are numerous records in archives, both in England and in Canada, that will give information on individual participants in the War of 1812. Please remember that the key to locating the records of a veteran is a knowledge of the regiment or ship, because the records are filed by regiment or ship, with no overall index being available. The last five references in the previous section will be of inestimable assistance to you as you seek your ancestor who was a veteran of this conflict. Be sure and make good use of them. As of 1812-15, it is well to remember that most of the so-called Canadian military records are essentially British and therefore the major repositories for them are in England. The best place to go for archival records of the War of 1812 is the Public Record Office in London, the second best place is the National Archives of Canada in Ottawa. The military sections in the following reference volume will describe to you the records available in the British Public Record Office.

___A. Bevan and A. Duncan, TRACING YOUR ANCESTORS IN THE PUBLIC RECORD OFFICE, Her Majesty's Stationery Office, London, England, 1990, see sections on soldiers, sailors, and marines.

There are also records in Canadian repositories, but many of the more valuable ones are copies of those in England. A good overview of the records available in Canadian archives is:

___S. Sutherland, CANADIAN ARCHIVAL SOURCES AND THE WAR OF 1812, in W. J. Welsh and D. C. Skaggs, WAR ON THE GREAT LAKES, Kent State University Press, Kent, OH, 1991, pages 93-99.

The National Archives of Canada is located at 395 Wellington Street, Ottawa, Ontario, Canada K1A 0N3. The telephone number is 1-(613)-995-5138. The holdings of this repository, including the military records, are described in:

___J. Roy, TRACING YOUR ANCESTORS IN CANADA, National Archives of Canada, Ottawa, Ontario, Canada, 1991.

There are available in the National Archives of Canada two major record collections: (1) the record groups RG which are Canadian government records, and (2) the manuscript groups MG which are copies of British government records and personal papers. Record Group 8, referred to as RG8, deals with the military in Canada for about a hundred years, 1790-1890. The major volumes in this RG8 for War-of-1812 searching are:

___Record Group 8, RG8, National Archives of Canada, Series C, BOOKS PERTINENT TO THE WAR OF 1812, Book Numbers 19-26 (officers' memorials), 187-222 (officers' half-pay), 187-222 and 496-504 (pensioners), 505-510 (petitions for relief), 676-688 and 688A-688E (officers' letter books), 1218-1227 (headquarters letter books).

Record Group 9, referred to as RG9, has the records of the Department of Militia and Defense, 1776-1922:

__Record Group 9, RG9, National Archives of Canada, MILITIA
RECORDS, officers, muster rolls, correspondence, orders.
In the manuscript groups, the microfilm copies of the British War Office
records are the most promising for genealogical information:
__Manuscript Group 13, Copies of British War Office Records, National
Archives of Canada, WAR OFFICE PAPERS DEALING WITH THE
WAR OF 1812, muster books and pay lists, description and succession
books (give information on the men in each regiment), Series WO 17
(monthly returns), WO 28 (orders), WO 44 (artillery), WO 55 (engi-
neers).

The pertinent branch of the Public Record Office in London is the
one located at Ruskin Avenue, Kew, Richmond, Surrey TW9 4DU. The
major records there for the War of 1812 are the ones listed above plus the
following:
__War Office Record Groups, British Public Record Office, RECORDS
PERTINENT TO THE WAR OF 1812, WO 10-13 (muster books and
pay lists), WO 17 (monthly returns), WO 25 (casualty lists). Also see
Admiralty Record Group ADM 37 (muster rolls for ships), and ADM
31-35 (pay books for ships).

The provincial archives in the areas that were populated in the War
of 1812 also have records of the War. The most important of these
archives are the following:
__The Provincial Archives of Ontario, 77 Grenville Street, Toronto,
Ontario, Canada M7A 2R9. Telephone 1-(416)-327-1553. See J. B.
Gilchrist, THE ONTARIO ARCHIVES, RECORDS AND RESEARCH
METHODS, Families 15, No. 4 (1976) 168-76, and Toronto Area
Archivists Group, GUIDE TO ARCHIVES IN THE TORONTO
AREA, The Group, Toronto, Ontario, Canada, 1978. The National
Archives of Canada holds the land petitions for Ontario (Upper
Canada) during 1791-1867, with a surname index. The National
Archives of Canada also has records of military pensions granted 1814-
67 (Record Group 9). Also see PENSIONERS OF THE WAR OF
1812,, The Ontario Register 1, No. 4 (1968) and 4, No.2 (1971).
__Archives Nationales de Quebec, 1210 avenue du Seminaire, Sainte-Foy,
Quebec, Canada G1V 4N1. Telephone: 1-(418)-644-4482. Especially
look into Army and Militia Correspondence (1770-1865), petitions for
lands made by militiamen (1812-51), and family dossiers.
__Public Archives of Nova Scotia, 6016 University Avenue, Halifax, Nova
Scotia, Canada B3H 1W4. Telephone: 1-(902)-424-6060. For military
holdings in Record Group 27, see INVENTORY OF MANUSCRIPTS
IN THE PUBLIC ARCHIVES OF NOVA SCOTIA, The Archives,
Halifax, Nova Scotia, Canada, 1976. Especially look into veterans'
petitions for land grants (with surname index) and the lists of British
military officers stationed in Nova Scotia.

__Provincial Archives of New Brunswick, Bonar Law Building, University of New Brunswick, Fredricton, New Brunswick, Canada E3B 5H1. Telephone: 1-(506)-453-2122. See A. B. Rigby, A GUIDE TO THE MANUSCRIPT COLLECTIONS IN THE PROVINCIAL ARCHIVES OF NEW BRUNSWICK, The Archives, Fredricton, New Brunswick, Canada, 1977. See also the inventory of the New Brunswick Museum, which has a good manuscript collection: INVENTORY OF MANU-SCRIPTS, The New Brunswick Museum, St. Johns, New Brunswick, Canada, 1967. Do not overlook the petitions for land grants (1784–1845).

__Public Archives of Newfoundland and Labrador, Colonial Building, Military Road, St. Johns, Newfoundland, Canada A1C 2C9. Telephone: 1-(709)-729-3065.

As mentioned briefly above, land grant records are an excellent source for discovering an ancestor's military service. Following military service, a veteran could submit a petition for land to the Lieutenant Governor of the province in which he lived. Upon approval, a warrant for the land was issued, a survey was made, and then a patent or grant was given. These records remain in the provincial archives which are listed just above. The most valuable of these records are the petitions, because they often give the name of the petitioner, his age, his marital status, number of children, length of residence in the province, former residences, and past service to the government. This last item will reveal military service. Most of the petitions in the provincial archives are filed alphabet-ically or they are indexed, so they are therefore easy to search. Written inquiries for index searches may be addressed to the relevant archives. Be sure to enclose a self-addressed envelope and an international reply coupon.

Books by George K. Schweitzer

CIVIL WAR GENEALOGY. A 78-paged book of 316 sources for tracing your Civil War ancestor. Chapters include [I]: The Civil War, [II]: The Archives, [III]: National Publications, [IV]: State Publications, [V]: Local Sources, [VI]: Military Unit Histories, [VII]: Civil War Events.

GEORGIA GENEALOGICAL RESEARCH. A 235-paged book containing 1303 sources for tracing your GA ancestor along with detailed instructions. Chapters include [I]: GA Background, [II]: Types of Records, [III]: Record Locations, [IV]: Research Procedure and County Listings (detailed listing of records available for each of the 159 GA counties).

GERMAN GENEALOGICAL RESEARCH. A 252-paged book containing 1924 sources for tracing your German ancestor along with detailed instructions. Chapters include [I]: German Background, [II]: Germans to America, [III]: Bridging the Atlantic, [IV]: Types of German Records, [V]: German Record Repositories, [VI]: The German Language.

HANDBOOK OF GENEALOGICAL SOURCES. A 217-paged book describing all major and many minor sources of genealogical information with precise and detailed instructions for obtaining data from them. 129 sections going from adoptions, archives, atlases---down through gazetteers, group theory, guardianships---to War of 1812, ward maps, wills, and WPA records.

KENTUCKY GENEALOGICAL RESEARCH. A 154-paged book containing 1191 sources for tracing your KY ancestor along with detailed instructions. Chapters include [I]: KY Background, [II]: Types of Records, [III]: Record Locations, [IV]: Research Procedure and County Listings (detailed listing of records available for each of the 120 KY counties).

MARYLAND GENEALOGICAL RESEARCH. A 208-paged book containing 1176 sources for tracing your MD ancestor along with detailed instructions. Chapters include [I]: MD Background, [II]: Types of Records, [III]: Record Locations, [IV]: Research Procedure and County Listings (detailed listing of records available for each of the 23 MD counties and for Baltimore City).

MASSACHUSETTS GENEALOGICAL RESEARCH. A 279–paged book containing 1709 sources for tracing your MA ancestor along with detailed instructions. Chapters include [I]: MA Background, [II]: Types of Records, [III]: Record Locations, [IV]: Research Procedure and County-Town-City Listings (detailed listing of records available for each of the 14 MA counties and the 351 cities-towns).

NEW YORK GENEALOGICAL RESEARCH. A 240-paged book containing 1426 sources for tracing your NY ancestor along with detailed instructions. Chapters include [I]: NY Background, [II]: Types of Records, [III]: Record Locations, [IV]: Research Procedure and NY City Record Listings (detailed listing of records available for the 5 counties of NY City), [V]: Record Listings for Other Counties (detailed listing of records available for each of the other 57 NY counties).

NORTH CAROLINA GENEALOGICAL RESEARCH. A 172–paged book containing 1233 sources for tracing your NC ancestor along with detailed instructions. Chapters include [I]: NC Background, [II]: Types of Records, [III]: Record Locations, [IV]: Research Procedure and County Listings (detailed listing of records available for each of the 100 NC counties).

OHIO GENEALOGICAL RESEARCH. A 225-paged book containing 1241 sources for tracing your OH ancestor along with detailed instructions. Chapters include [I]: OH Background, [II]: Types of Records, [III]: Record Locations, [IV]: Research Procedure and County Listings (detailed listing of records available for each of the 88 OH counties).

PENNSYLVANIA GENEALOGICAL RESEARCH. A 225-paged book containing 1309 sources for tracing your PA ancestor along with detailed instructions. Chapters include [I]: PA Background, [II]: Types of Records, [III]: Record Locations, [IV]: Research Procedure and County Listings (detailed listing of records available for each of the 67 PA counties).

REVOLUTIONARY WAR GENEALOGY. A 110-paged book containing 407 sources for tracing your Revolutionary War ancestor. Chapters include [I]: Revolutionary War History, [II]: The Archives, [III]: National Publications, [IV]: State Publications, [V]: Local Sources, [VI]: Military Unit Histories, VII: Sites and Museums.

SOUTH CAROLINA GENEALOGICAL RESEARCH. A 190-paged book containing 1107 sources for tracing your SC ancestor along with detailed instructions. Chapters include [I]: SC Background, [II]: Types of Records, [III]: Record Locations, [IV]: Research Procedure and County Listings (detailed listing of records available for each of the 47 SC counties and districts).

TENNESSEE GENEALOGICAL RESEARCH. A 136-paged book containing 1073 sources for tracing your TN ancestor along with detailed instructions. Chapters include [I]: TN Background, [II]: Types of Records, [III]: Record Locations, [IV]: Research Procedure and County Listings (detailed listing of records available for each of the 96 TN counties).

VIRGINIA GENEALOGICAL RESEARCH. A 187-paged book containing 1273 sources for tracing your VA ancestor along with detailed instructions. Chapters include [I]: VA Background, [II]: Types of Records, [III]: Record Locations, [IV]: Research Procedure and County Listings (detailed listing of records available for each of the 100 VA counties and 41 major cities).

WAR OF 1812 GENEALOGY. A 75-paged book of 289 sources for tracing your War of 1812 ancestor. Chapters include [I]: History of the War, [II]: Service Records, [III]: Post-War Records, [IV]: Publications, [V]: Local Sources, [VI]: Sites and Events, VII: Sources for British and Canadian Participants.

All of the above books may be ordered from Dr. Geo. K. Schweitzer, 407 Ascot Court, Knoxville, TN 37923-5807. Or send a long SASE for a FREE descriptive leaflet on any or all of the books.